MODERN CHINA

A Volume in the Comparative Societies Series

MODERN CHINA

A Volume in the Comparative Societies Series

RICHARD E. BARRETT
University of Illinois at Chicago

FANG LI
The University of Chicago

HAROLD R. KERBO, Series Editor
California Polytechnic State University

McGraw-Hill College

Boston,   Burr Ridge, IL   Dubuque, IA   Madison,WI
New York   San Francisco   St. Louis
Bangkok Bogotá Caracas Lisbon London Madrid Mexico City
Milan New Delhi Seoul Singapore Sydney Taipei Toronto

McGraw-Hill College

A Division of The **McGraw·Hill** Companies

MODERN CHINA

This book is printed on acid-free paper.

3 4 5 6 7 8 9 0 DOC/DOC 3

ISBN 0-07-292826-3

Editorial director: *Phillip A. Butcher*
Sponsoring editor: *Sally Constable*
Marketing manager: *Leslie A. Kraham*
Project manager: *Kimberly D. Hooker*
Production associate: *Debra R. Benson*
Senior designer: *Michael Warrell*
Cover image: © *Christian Michaels. Courtesy FPG International.*
Compositor: *Shepherd, Inc.*
Typeface: *10/12 Palatino*
Printer: *R. R. Donnelley & Sons Company*

Library of Congress Cataloging-in-Publication Data
Barrett, Richard E.
   Modern China / Richard E. Barrett, Fang Li.
     p.   cm. — (Comparative societies series)
   Includes bibliographical references and index.
   ISBN 0-07-292826-3 (alk. paper)
     1. China—Social conditions—1976-   2. China—Social life and
    customs—1976-   I. Li, Fang.   II. Title.   III. Series.
  HN733.5.B38   1999
  306'.0951—dc21

98-44545

http://www.mhhe.com

EDITOR'S PREFACE

In one of the early scenes of the movie *Reds*, the US revolutionary journalist John Reed, just back from covering the beginning of World War I,
is asked by a roomful of business leaders, "What is this War really
about?" John Reed stands, and stops all conversation with a one word
reply—"profits." Today, war between major industrial nations would
disrupt profits much more than create money for a military industrial
complex. Highly integrated global markets and infrastructures support
the daily life of suburban families in Chicago and urban squatter settlements in Bombay. These ties produce a social and economic ecology that
transcends political and cultural boundaries.

The world is a very different place than it was for our parents and
grandparents. Those rare epic events of world war certainly invaded
their everyday lives and futures, but we now find that daily events
thousands of miles away, in countries large and small, have a greater
impact on North Americans than ever before, with the speed of this impact multiplied many times in recent decades. Our standard of living,
jobs, and even prospects of living in a healthy environment have never
before been so dependent on outside forces.

Yet, there is much evidence that North Americans have less easy
access to good information about the outside world than even a few
years ago. Since the end of the Cold War, newspaper and television coverage of events in other countries has dropped dramatically. It is difficult
to put much blame on the mass media, however: international news seldom sells any more. There is simply less interest.

It is not surprising, then, that Americans know comparatively little
about the outside world. A recent *Los Angeles Times* survey provides a
good example: People in eight countries were asked five basic questions
about current events of the day. Americans were dead last in their knowledge, trailing people from Canada, Mexico, England, France, Spain, Germany, and Italy.* It is also not surprising that the annual report published
by the Swiss World Economic Forum always ranks American executives
quite low in their international experience and understanding.

Such ignorance harms American competitiveness in the world economy in many ways. But there is much more. Seymour Martin Lipset put it
nicely in one of his recent books: "Those who know only one country know
no country" (Lipset 1996: 17). Considerable time spent in a foreign country
is one of the best stimulants for a sociological imagination: Studying or

---

*For example, while only 3 percent of Germans missed all five questions, 37 percent of the
    Americans did (*Los Angeles Times*, March 16, 1994).

doing research in other countries makes us realize how much we really, in fact, have learned about our own society in the process. Seeing other social arrangements, ways of doing things, and foreign perspectives allows for far greater insight to the familiar, our own society. This is also to say that ignorance limits solutions to many of our own serious social problems. How many Americans, for example, are aware that levels of poverty are much lower in all other advanced nations and that the workable government services in those countries keep poverty low? Likewise, how many Americans are aware of alternative means of providing health care and quality education or reducing crime?

We can take heart in the fact that sociology in the United States has become more comparative in recent decades. A comparative approach, of course, was at the heart of classical European sociology during the 1800s. But as sociology was transported from Europe to the United States early in the 20th century, it lost much of this comparative focus. In recent years, sociology journals have published more comparative research. There are large data sets with samples from many countries around the world in research seeking general laws on issues such as the causes of social mobility or political violence, all very much in the tradition of Durkheim. But we also need much more of the old Max Weber. His was a qualitative historical and comparative perspective (Smelser 1976; Ragin and Zaret 1983). Weber's methodology provides a richer understanding of other societies, a greater recognition of the complexity of social, cultural, and historical forces shaping each society. Ahead of his time in many ways, C. Wright Mills was planning a qualitative comparative sociology of world regions just before his death in 1961 (Horowitz 1983: 324). [Too few American sociologists have yet to follow in his footsteps.]

Following these trends, sociology textbooks in the United States have also become more comparative in content in recent years. And while this tendency must be applauded, it is not enough. Typically there is an example from Japan here, another from Germany there, and so on haphazardly for a few countries in different subject areas as the writer's knowledge of these bits and pieces allows. What we need are the textbook equivalents of a richer Weberian comparative analysis, a qualitative comparative analysis of the social, cultural, and historical forces that have combined to make relatively unique societies around the world. It is this type of comparative material that can best help people in the United States overcome their lack of understanding about other countries and allow them to see their own society with much greater insight.

The Comparative Societies Series, of which this book is a part, has been designed as a small step in filling this need. We have currently selected 12 countries on which to focus: Japan, Thailand, Switzerland, Mexico, Eritria, Hungary, Germany, China, India, Iran, Brazil, and Russia. We selected these countries as representatives of major world regions and cultures, and each will be examined in separate books written by talented sociologists. All of the basic sociological issues and topics will be covered: Each book will begin with a look at the important historical and geographical forces shaping the society, then turn to basic aspects of social organization and culture. From there each book will proceed to examine the political and economic institutions of the specific country, along with the social stratification, the family, religion, education, and finally urbanization, demography, social problems, and social change.

Although each volume in the Comparative Societies Series is of necessity brief to allow for use as supplementary readings in standard sociology courses, we have tried to assure that this brief coverage provides students with sufficient information to better understand each society, as well as their own. The ideal would be to transport every student to another country for a period of observation and learning. Realizing the unfortunate impracticality of this ideal, we hope to do the next best thing—to at least mentally move these students to a country very different from their own, provide something of the everyday reality of the people in these other countries, and demonstrate how the tools of sociological analysis can help them see these societies as well as their own with much greater understanding.

Harold R. Kerbo
San Luis Obispo, CA
June 1997

China has experienced more rapid social change than almost any other nation over the last century. From a largely peasant economy, it has become one of the world's new industrial powers. This has not been without tremendous cost; external invasion, internal disorder, and bad policy decisions have cost the lives of tens of millions and led to great suffering for untold others.

What kind of society exists in China today? In many senses it is a very *transitional* society: The forces that have been unleashed by rapid economic growth over the past two decades are shaking the foundations of the Communist state that has existed since 1949. Young people today have very different life goals and life chances than those in 1968 or in 1948. One purpose of this book is to give sufficient description of the current state of China's society that the reader can understand why many young people are making the kinds of choices that they do.

Sociology is not only interested in very broad changes in social life, but also in how the daily life of individuals may vary within a society or between societies. We have decided to focus on a few topics—whether or not to start a business, how labor markets operate, housing in urban areas, sexuality and gender, how to find a mate—and to show some of the special characteristics of the Chinese solutions to these universal problems. Of course, the more we investigated these topics, the more we found that supposedly Chinese practices were in a state of rapid evolution themselves.

Throughout this book, we will be struggling with several possible interpretations of why China has its current form of social organization and why Chinese act the way they do. In general, we do not hold to a theory of Chinese cultural uniqueness. China has absorbed many foreign faiths, including Buddhism, Islam, Christianity, and Marxism; and they have had remarkable effects on Chinese culture and social structure. However, we recognize that the ways in which China has been modernizing (especially after 1949) represent an adaptation of foreign systems to China's social and physical ecology and to a traditional set of personal and family relations that still have a major impact on Chinese today.

It must also be recognized that the world surrounding China has changed dramatically over the past half-century. China has "stood up," in Chairman Mao's 1949 phrase, and is no longer a weak and disorganized state open to foreign depredations. On the other hand, the heretofore insular Chinese economy is increasingly linked to the world economy, and international economic trends have the power to affect even remote corners of Chinese society. China has benefited from what Alexander Gerschenkron called the "advantages of backwardness," in that it can jump ahead without replicating each stage of development of nations that industrialized at an earlier point. Yet because of this discontinuity, social and economic institutions in China often mesh poorly with each other. Jumping from the abacus to the personal computer, as many Chinese did, is not without its costs.

We have benefited from the insights of many scholars (both Chinese and foreign) over the years; two deserve particular mention, both as mentors and colleagues: Martin K. Whyte and William L. Parish. Richard Barrett would like to thank his wife, Teresa Chou; his two older daughters, Kristin and Emily, for helping with the index; and his youngest daughter Sarah for amiable distraction. Fang Li would like to thank his wife Nathalie for her support throughout the project. One final point: the pronunciations given after the Chinese terms are only a rough approximation of actual Chinese pronunciations, and teachers and students are encouraged to check with native speakers as to how these terms are spoken in *putonghua*.

Richard E. Barrett
Fang Li

CONTENTS

Chapter 6

Chapter 7

Chapter 8

Chapter 11

MODERN CHINA

A Volume in the Comparative Societies Series

China and Its Asian Neighbors

RUSSIA

KAZAKHSTAN

Lake Baikal

Lake Balkhash

KYRGYZSTAN

MONGOLIA

• Karamay

• Yining

• Urumqi

AFG

• Kashgar   Xinjiang

PAK.

Yumen •

• Hailar

Heilongjiang

• Qiqihar   • Harbin

• Changchun

Nei Mongol   Jilin

Shenyang

Liaoning

NORTH KOREA

Hohhot •   Beijing •   Dalian

Tianjin •

SOUTH KOREA

Golmud •   Xining •

Yinchuan •

Ningxia

Taiyuan •   Shijiazhuang •

Shanxi

• Yantai

• Qingdao

Jinan •

Shandong

Yellow Sea

Qinghai

Lanzhou •

Gansu

Xi'an •

Shaanxi

Zhengzhou •

Henan

Jiangsu

Anhui

Nanjing •

Hefei •   Shanghai

Hangzhou •

Xizang

Sichuan

Hubei

Wuhan •

Chengdu •   Chongqing •

Zhejiang

Lhasa •

NEPAL

BHUTAN

INDIA

BANGLADESH

Changsha •

Hunan

Nanchang •

Jiangxi

East China Sea

Guizhou •

Guiyang •

Fuzhou •

Fujian

Xiamen •

Taibei •

TAIWAN

Kunming •

Yunnan

Guangxi

Nanning •

Guangdong

Guangzhou •

Hong Kong •

MYANMAR   VIETNAM

LAOS

Bay of Bengal

Haikou •

Hainan

South China Sea

THAILAND

CAMBODIA

PHILIPPINES

China

⊕ National Capital

Xi'an •   City

International Boundary

Provincial Boundary

Hunan   Province Name

- - - Disputed Boundary

500 km

0   500 Miles

The People, the Place, and the Past

INTRODUCTION

In the recent past, the justification for studying China might have been that it was a unique social system in which about one-fifth of the world's population lived in virtual isolation. The past two decades, and especially the past few years, have changed all that. The range of contacts between China and the United States has expanded enormously. China has also become an important actor on the international scene as well.

In the five years between 1993 and 1997, the Chinese economy has grown at a rate of about 11 percent per year (*People's Daily*, March 3, 1998: 1). This average annual growth rate is far higher than that of **developed nations** (2.2 percent) or **less-developed nations** (6.3 percent), or of the United States (2.9 percent) or Japan (1.4 percent) during the 1993–97 period. In fact, China had the highest growth rate of any nation on the globe during this period, a remarkable feat for such a large and diverse nation.

This level of economic growth has given China great economic strength. By 1995, estimates of China's gross domestic product (a measure of all the goods and services produced and consumed there) stood at U.S. $698 billion. This was well behind the GDP in the United States ($6.952 trillion) or Japan ($5.109 trillion), but about even with Brazil ($688 billion) and well ahead of such major nations as Russia ($345 billion) or India ($324 billion).

The East Asian regions, particularly those with residents of Chinese origin, are also notable for another aspect of economic strength: their deep pockets. The nation with the highest 1997 foreign currency reserves was Japan, at U.S. $221 billion. China stood second, at $140 billion. Hong Kong (now a part of China) was at $93 billion, Taiwan was at $83 billion, and Singapore's reserves were $74 billion. By way of contrast, Germany had foreign currency reserves of $82 billion, and the United States' were $69 billion. While there is a current tendency (based on economic problems in Thailand, Korea, and Indonesia) to view the East Asian economies as unstable, the parts of East Asia peopled by Chinese and Japanese have shown a remarkable ability to combine high savings rates with high rates of economic development, regardless of the political system.

What Do We Mean by Chinese?

Who are the Chinese? Clearly, Chinese culture and the nation-state that we recognize as China are two different concepts. Chinese culture includes a far-flung group of people with a distinctive set of eating habits, religious practices, and family and social organization. It includes Chinese people living under a great variety of forms of political organization, levels of economic development, and degrees of urbanization and industrialization.

The nation-state of China (and here, for simplicity's sake, we will only consider the mainland part of the People's Republic of China, not the island of Taiwan) includes 1.131 billion people; 91 million of these people (or about 8 percent of the population of China) are called **national minorities** and are culturally quite distinct from the Chinese, or **Han,** majority population (1990 census data; see Population Census Office 1993a: 300). Thus the span of Chinese culture is both wider and narrower than the borders of the nation-state, not unlike that of the culture of the United States.

China is, in fact, a useful nation to study because this inexact overlap between cultural unit and nation-state is a much more common state of affairs in many nations than is usually supposed. The boundaries between cultures and nation-states can change over centuries, or even blend to form new political or cultural amalgams.

National Minorities in China

Over hundreds and sometimes thousands of years, the Han people, whom we think of as Chinese, have been in close contact with their neighbors. Some groups have been almost totally assimilated into the Han, while others have remained culturally distinct. These national minorities totaled about 90 million people in 1990, or about 7–8 percent of China's population. Fifty-five groups are recognized as national minorities; of these, 18 groups had more than 1 million members, and 13 groups had fewer than 20,000 members (Banister 1992c). One largely Han group, China's Muslims, is also classified as a national minority (the Hui minority). A number of other minority groups are also Muslim, but they are classified by their ethnic background and language, such as the Kazakhs and Uighurs, rather than by their religion.

A number of these minority groups are growing rapidly because until recently they were excluded from birth planning limits (Poston and Jing 1987). With the exception of China's Korean minority, most minority peoples lag behind the majority Han on such social indicators as education, income, and longevity. China's national minorities are scattered throughout the country but are concentrated near China's borders. In recent years, significant numbers of Han Chinese have moved into national minority areas for reasons of national defense or economic development, but there is little indication of assimilation, especially of much intermarriage, on either side in these regions.

Who or What Else Is Chinese?

There are several other parts of the globe that are Chinese and a large number of residents of other nations who would describe themselves (or be described by others) as Chinese.

Taiwan

This island, about the size of Connecticut and Massachusetts combined, has been settled by Chinese since the seventeenth century. It gradually became absorbed into China but was awarded to Japan at the conclusion of the Sino-Japanese war (Barclay 1954; Clough 1982). A colony of Japan from 1895–1945, it was taken over by the Nationalist Chinese state at the end of World War II and has remained as a separate entity apart from the People's Republic since 1949, even though it is claimed by China as a province.

Since 1965, Taiwan has experienced very rapid economic development, and since the mid-1980s, rapid political development toward democratization. As a result of one of the world's most successful and noncoercive birth control programs, Taiwan now has a population of about 20 million people with a standard of living on a par with nations like Italy. Among all developing nations, it has been among the most successful at combining rapid economic growth with an equitable distribution of income (Barrett and Whyte 1982; Fei, Ranis and Kuo 1979).

As the majority of native Taiwanese (descendants of those Chinese migrants arriving before 1895) have gained political power through democratic means at the expense of the **Nationalist Party** *(Kuomintang),* they have begun to wrestle with whether Taiwan should once again become part of China or become an independent state. China has proposed a "one nation, two systems" solution, allowing Taiwan to keep its own economic system for a time, after political reintegration; and China has refused to rule out the use of force to recover the wayward province.

Taiwanese culture is similar to that found in the place of origin of most of its southern Chinese ancestors, that is, the Minnan people of southern Fujian province and the Hakka people of the border between Fujian and Guangdong provinces. Yet due to more than a century of separation—first as a Japanese colony, then as the sole province of the Republic of China—it has developed faster economically and in quite different ways from the rest of China. The collision between the view of the People's Republic of China (that Taiwan should be integrated into the motherland) and that of the majority of people in Taiwan (that the island would put its economic prosperity and democratic freedoms at risk in a merger with an authoritarian state) has the continuing potential for serious political and military conflict.

Hong Kong

A British colony from the 1840s to 1997, Hong Kong experienced very rapid economic growth between 1950 and the present (Welsh 1996) and was reintegrated into China as a Special Administrative Region in 1997. According to the treaty turning Hong Kong over to China, the former colony is to be allowed to maintain its special economic structure and legal systems (which give considerably more protection to private property, human rights, and freedom of expression than does the legal system of the People's Republic of China) for the next 50 years. Hong Kong has a population of just under 6 million people crowded into one of the densest cities in the world. The vast majority of Hong Kong's residents (over 97 percent) are of Chinese origin, and most of them are from neighboring Guangdong province.

Both Hong Kong and Taiwan are significant to China's recent economic development because they have been models of successful capitalist development and major sources of investment capital, technology transfer, and general knowledge about how the world economic system works. They also have had a profound influence on the rise of consumerism and the youth culture: Many Taiwanese or Hong Kong singers rapidly develop large followings in the rest of China. Much of the Western, especially American, culture that has been absorbed into China first received a distinctive Chinese spin in Hong Kong or Taiwan before it became popular there.

Singapore

This largely Chinese city-state, one of the largest ports in the world, is another legacy of the British Empire. Located on the strategic Strait of Malacca, this former entrepôt city has grown into a high-technology center focusing on finance, manufacturing, and petroleum processing (Yue 1985). Over three-quarters of its 2.9 million residents are Chinese, and the state has been independent since 1959. It is governed by a one-party, authoritarian state. The People's Republic of China makes no territorial claim on Singapore, and this state is a major source of investment capital for industries in China. The Chinese who migrated to Singapore from the nineteenth century on came from a number of different parts of south China. Like Hong Kong, it has had high rates of economic growth and a high standard of living.

The Overseas Chinese

Migrants from China can be found in almost any part of the world, but they have their greatest concentration in Southeast Asia and in North

America and Australia. The ancestors of most of today's **Overseas Chinese** originated in various parts of South China. The Overseas Chinese are particularly important in Southeast Asian nations, where they often have had a major impact on the economy. In many instances, Chinese became the "middleman minorities" (those who handled small and, later, big business tasks) in the colonial empires of European nations, and they have continued to play a key role after independence as well.

Large numbers of Chinese came to the American West to mine for gold and to build railroads. Racial discrimination in housing and occupation forced Chinese to live in densely populated "Chinatowns"; many specialized in service activities like restaurants and laundries. Since the mid-1960s, when racist immigration quotas were finally overthrown in both the United States and Canada, many Chinese have migrated to both nations, often settling in such cities as Vancouver, Seattle, San Francisco, Los Angeles, Chicago, Toronto, and New York.

Many recent and better-educated Chinese migrants live throughout these metropolitan areas and are found in a variety of occupations. Yet Chinese gangs, called *snakeheads,* still take advantage of the desperation of many Chinese to get to North America, smuggling them in for huge sums of money. Many illegal Chinese migrants end up working off debts to these gangsters in sweatshops or restaurants, learning almost no English and fearful of going to the authorities.

While Chinese migration to Australia (a favorite destination of many Hong Kong émigrés) has also become common over the past two decades, fewer Chinese have migrated to Europe, western Asia, South America, or Africa. The number of Overseas Chinese throughout the world was estimated to be about 27 million people in the early 1980s; of that total, about 20 million lived in Southeast Asia (Poston and Yu 1992: 122–32). In the United States in 1990, over a half million people were migrants from China, another 147,000 were migrants from Hong Kong, 244,000 were migrants from Taiwan, and 222,000 were Chinese migrants from another country (Anderton, Barrett, and Bogue 1997: 387–9).

There are several reasons why the Overseas Chinese form a special immigrant group. In several Asian nations, they are the only major immigrant group and have suffered from various kinds of discrimination, including denial of citizenship (the Philippines), mass expulsion (many of the "boat people" refugees of the 1970s from Vietnam were Overseas Chinese), or ethnic pogroms (as many as a half-million Chinese may have been massacred in Indonesia in the mid-1960s). Various forms of legal and extra-legal discrimination against Chinese, especially in terms of forced residential segregation, were common in the United States or Canada (Spence 1990: 213–14).

The Overseas Chinese have often maintained a deep interest in China and Chinese culture. They were a major source of money and support for agitation against the Qing dynasty in the early twentieth century through the Revolutionary Alliance (Tong-meng-hui) of Sun Yat-sen

(1866–1925), the forerunner to the Nationalist Party (Spence 1990: 262). Since 1979, the Overseas Chinese have been the major source of foreign investment in China (LaCroix and Plummer 1995). They have also played a major part in China's export success by identifying new markets and helping infant Chinese industries to develop products that meet international standards of quality and style.

Finally, the Overseas Chinese retain great pride in their culture and civilization, even though they often have no plans to ever return to China. More than 1.3 million Americans reported speaking a dialect of Chinese at home (Anderton et al. 1997: 399), and many educated Chinese migrants virtually require that their children learn the language.

THE SOCIAL ECOLOGY OF CHINA

Chinese society is shaped by its geography. Its 9.6 million square kilometers of area (it is larger than the United States and slightly smaller than Canada) stretch across 5,000 kilometers of Asia. Its perimeter is almost evenly divided between land borders with North Korea, Russia, Mongolia, Kazakhstan, Kirghizstan, Tajikstan, Afghanistan, Pakistan, India Nepal, Bhutan, Burma, Laos, and Vietnam (a total of 20,000 kilometers) and coastlines bordering the Gulf of Tonkin, the South China Sea, the East China Sea, the Yellow Sea (Huang Hai), and the Bohai Gulf (18,000 kilometers; see the map on page xviii and Federal Research Division 1988: 62–72).

Population settlement in China is a study in contrasts. Many rural areas have a population density as high as some cities or towns in the United States, while the desolate high plateaus of Tibet and Qinghai and the deserts of Xinjiang (all in China's far west) are almost unpopulated but for nomadic herders. More than 90 percent of the population lives on little more than one-third of China's land area. Aside from China's high plateaus and deserts, which are virtually useless for agriculture, a number of mountain chains and hill ranges cut across central and southern China, impeding transportation and concentrating agriculture in river valleys. Both of China's two greatest rivers, the Huang He (the Yellow River, the cradle of Chinese civilization) in the north and the Chiang Jiang (referred to as the Yangtze River by Westerners) in central China are major east-west conduits of irrigation and transportation.

In terms of climate, most of China falls in the temperate zone. Since most of the population lives within a thousand kilometers (or usually less) of the seacoast, the East Asian monsoon air circulation (cool and dry in winter, hot and wet in summer) affects much of the country. Wheat is grown from the province of Henan north; south of that, rice predominates.

For many Chinese, altitude is destiny. The higher up the hill or mountainside you live, the more likely you are to have less education, to be in poverty, to have less access to medical care, and, overall, to have fewer chances in life. One of the surprises of empirical studies of the Chinese countryside in the 1970s by William Parish and Martin Whyte

(1978), among others, was the difference that existed in the incomes of farmers in nearby communes or production brigades. Farming households in a production brigade (usually the size of a village, or from a few hundred to a thousand people) growing paddy rice in a fertile river valley could often be making three or four times the annual income of a nearby production brigade growing sweet potatoes and peanuts on dry hillside fields.

Regions of China

Typically, Chinese provinces have a central plain region (with good agricultural land) surrounded by hills, then by mountain ridges that form the boundary with the next province. These physical barriers have, over the centuries, become cultural and economic barriers as well (Skinner 1964, 1965). Most of China's provinces have a distinctive dialect of the Chinese language that is often not very intelligible to people from the next province; sometimes, the dialects differ from county to county. While the Chinese language is written in the same way everywhere, and Chinese spoken grammar is fairly similar everywhere, the sounds of provincial or county dialects can differ a great deal. Some of these dialects may be partial survivals of Chinese speech of past eras; the Minnan dialect of Taiwan and southern Fujian province, for example, may be a partial survival of the Chinese language of the Tang dynasty (sixth through tenth centuries AD).

The government of the People's Republic has tried to unify China by using one widely spoken northern dialect called *putonghua* (pronounced poo-tohng-hwa), or common speech, as the standard language throughout China in schools, government communications, and the mass media. Apparently they thought that as people learned this dialect, they would cease to use their regional languages. Although most younger people and all educated people speak and understand *putonghua*, usually called Mandarin by foreigners, the local dialects have shown a surprising degree of resiliency. Just as in the United States, people all over China seem to like their local dialects and are happy to teach them to their children. Dialect differences, like ethnicity, appear to be one of those areas where sociologists have generally "bet wrong" on the appeal of national standardization versus the desire for the preservation of local history and group uniqueness.

Over centuries, Chinese food habits have also developed a distinctly regional and provincial style. The Chinese themselves refer to a Hunan [province] restaurant or a Beijing duck restaurant. Hunan and Sichuan provincial cuisines are noted for their peppery dishes, Guangdong (Cantonese to Westerners) for its mild cuisine; and many northern provinces use wheat rather than rice as the key carbohydrate. Chinese have regional stereotypes of each other, just as Americans do: Shanghai people are supposed to be quick and commercial-minded, much like

Food is an important element in Chinese culture; relationships are often built or renewed over shared meals.

New Yorkers; whereas Beijing people are more like Bostonians—they see their city as the cultural hub of the universe.

Administratively speaking, the People's Republic of China rules over 32 provinces, municipalities, autonomous regions, or special administrative regions (see the map on p. 9), which are grouped into six large regions:

North: Beijing municipality, Tianjin municipality, Hebei province, Shanxi province, Inner Mongolia Autonomous Region.

Northeast: Liaoning province, Jilin province, Heilongjiang province.

East: Shanghai municipality, Jiangsu province, Zhejiang province, Anhui province, Fujian province, Jiangxi province, Shandong province.

Central-South: Henan province, Hubei province, Hunan province, Guangdong province, Guangxi-Zhuang Autonomous Region, Hainan province.

Southwest: Sichuan province, Chongqing municipality, Guizhou province, Yunnan province, Xizang Autonomous Region (Tibet).

Northwest: Shaanxi province, Gansu province, Qinghai province, Ningxia-Hui Autonomous Region, Xinjiang Autonomous Region.

In addition, Hong Kong is a Special Administrative Region. Taiwan, though not currently under control of the People's Republic of China, is

China's Province-Level Administrative Units

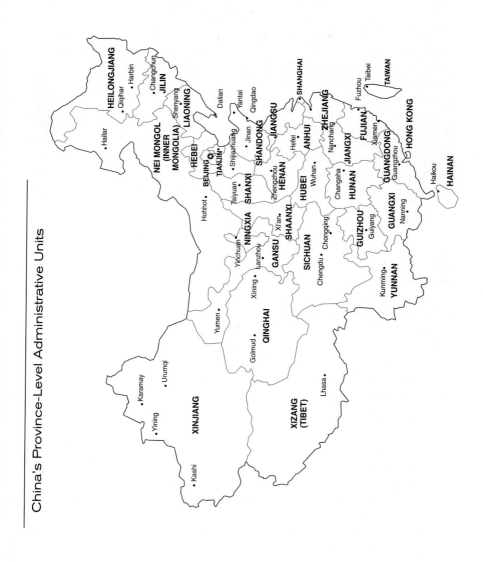

considered a province as well. Macau, a Portuguese colonial outpost near Hong Kong, is scheduled to revert to the People's Republic in 1999.

There are a number of other ways in which the area and population of China could be classified besides this administrative one. Many scholars divide the provinces of China into coastal, central, and western designations, on the grounds that these classifications more accurately reflect China's economic realities. In terms of population density, the coastal region provinces (including several inland provinces in the Chiang Jiang river area), with an average population density of at least 200 people per square kilometer, include Liaoning, Beijing, Tianjin, and Shanghai municipalities, Hebei, Shandong, Henan, Anhui, Jiangsu, Hubei, Jiangxi, Zhejiang, Hunan, Fujian, Guangdong, Hainan, and the Hong Kong Special Administrative Region. The central region provinces or autonomous regions, with population densities between 100 and 200 people per square kilometer, include Jilin, Shanxi, Shaanxi, Sichuan, Guizhou, and Guangxi-Zhuang. The western region provinces or autonomous regions, with population densities of less than 100 people per square kilometer, include Heilongjiang, Inner Mongolia, Gansu, Ningxia-Hui, Xinjiang, Qinghai, Xizang (Tibet), and Yunnan (Li 1992: 92).

The other way in which sociologists divide territories is by which populations are *functionally linked* to each other. Is an inhabitant of western Massachusetts more linked to Boston, to Hartford, Connecticut, or to New York City? This kind of functional linkage can be determined by flows of capital or labor, by cultural linkages, and by other factors. The functional linkage between Chinese cities and regions is only now being explored and appears to be rapidly changing under the impact of economic growth.

Religion in China

Aside from the adherents of Islam and Christianity (who never were more than a few percent of the whole population), most Chinese tended to take a syncretic view toward religion. Ancestor worship, local religious practices, Confucianism, Daoism, and Buddhism all tended to coexist in the minds of the believers and in the community.

Ancestor worship dates from at least three millennia ago and revolves around annual sacrifices at the grave sites of the ancestors. It could also often involve daily or monthly observances at the ancestor-altar within the home or at a temple owned by a clan or lineage who shared the same last name and original ancestors. The offering of incense, "spirit money," or food (the latter was then taken home and eaten by the practical Chinese) to the ancestors was supposed to supply their needs in the other world and to make them look with favor on the current generation. Local religious practice often involved propitiating (essentially bribing) the gods of a locality (such as the Tu Di Gong) or special-purpose gods (such as the Kitchen God, or the Mother-spirit of the Childbirth Bed, Chuang-mu Shen) who might otherwise cause trouble or give bad luck. Many of the Daoist spirits are only a cut above these gods; they are more like the Roman or Greek gods than the God of the Christian, Jew, or Muslim.

The perception that one is part of a network of ancestors and descendants as yet unborn meant that the individual had a great responsibility to others. **Confucianism,** or the thought of the philosopher Kong Zi (551–479 BC), was a system of thought designed to guide the individual in how to act to fulfill life's social roles. By fulfilling these roles, and acting in a proper manner, the ethical conduct of the individual was assured; if all acted in such a way, then the prosperity of the kingdom was also assured. While Confucian philosophers differed as to whether humans had a basically good or evil nature, with Meng Zi tending toward the former view, and the Legalists toward the latter (see Shinn and Worden 1988: 7–10), Confucians all supported the idea that learning, cultivation of the mind, harnessing the passions, and moderation in all things were essential to the improvement of the human condition.

The other side of the Chinese worldview is found in **Daoism** (Taoism), an equally ancient body of philosophical doctrines that says that nature is beyond human control. The individual has no responsibility to society; rather, "the goal of life for each individual is to find one's own personal adjustment to the rhythm of the natural (and the supernatural) world, to follow the Way (*dao*) of the universe" (Shinn and Worden 1988: 10). Much of Chinese mysticism—ranging from *kung fu* to numerology to alchemy—comes out of Daoism, and it has had a great influence on Chinese religious practice, art, and personal philosophy. This kind of individualism can range from the hermit who retreats to live in the bamboo grove to the spectacularly courageous pedestrian in the Beijing demonstrations of June 1989 who stopped a tank by refusing to move out of its way (see the photo in Spence 1990: 741).

Buddhism has been in China for more than a millennium and has also had a major influence on Chinese religious practice. A traditional Chinese funeral, for example, may have both Buddhist and Taoist elements; each of the religious specialists has his own area of expertise. All of these religious practices were attacked as superstition by Western missionaries and later by the Communist Party, which saw them as a waste of time and money and as part of the cultural superstructure of the old regime.

Religion never completely disappeared in post-1949 China; in many rural homes, the picture or bust of Mao was placed on the ancestor shrine in place of the forbidden ancestor tablets. Throughout China, the ancestors' grave sites were plowed under in the early 1950s (it had been estimated that 15 percent of China's farmland was devoted to graves) during the Land Reform campaigns. Yet burial grounds are making a modest comeback now. Some farmers or villages now allow nearby urban residents to bury the cremated remains of their relatives in graveyards (there is no space left for this in cities) and charge them for the upkeep of the site.

CHAPTER 1

   Organized, and nonorganized, religion is also making a comeback in both urban and rural areas, and it has attracted surprisingly little opposition from the government. One particularly popular religious movement is *qigong,* a breathing and exercise regimen that is supposed to improve health and can give the participant supernatural powers, including the ability to "heal the sick, fly through the air, and burn objects by touching them" (Kristof and WuDunn 1994: 133). These *qigong* masters enjoy large followings and put on performances much like faith healers in the United States.

AN OUTLINE OF CHINESE HISTORY

Since the known history of China is about 20 times longer than that of the United States, there appears to be a great deal more variation. (Table 1–1 presents a chronology of Chinese history.) Empires rise and fall; invasions succeed or are repulsed; the government is reorganized in a variety of ways. For most of these 4,000 years, there were two major systems of government. During the Xia, Shang, and Eastern and Western Chou dynasties (from about the twenty-first to the third century BC), China was a feudal state, with a hereditary nobility ruling over a vast mass of farmers. Government was decentralized, and wars between feudal rulers were common.

TABLE 1–1

Chronology of Chinese History

Time Period	Name of Era
Twenty-first–nineteenth century BC	Xia dynasty
Eighteenth–eleventh century BC	Shang dynasty
Tenth century–221 BC	Western and Eastern Chou dynasties
221–207 BC	Qin dynasty (Qin Shi Huangdi)
206 BC–9 AD	Western Han dynasty
25 AD–220 AD	Eastern Han dynasty
220–280 AD	Three Kingdoms period
265–316 AD	Western Jin dynasty
317–420 AD	Eastern Jin dynasty
420–588 AD	Southern and Northern dynasties
581–617 AD	Sui dynasty
518–907 AD	Tang dynasty
960–1279 AD	Song dynasty
1279–1368 AD	Yuan dynasty (Mongols)
1368–1644 AD	Ming dynasty
1644–1911 AD	Qing dynasty (Manchus)
1911–1949 AD	Republican period (*Kuomintang*/warlord rule)
1949 AD–present	People's Republic of China (Communist rule)

Many of the cultural elements that we think of as typically Chinese emerged during this period. A writing system using pictographs was developed for divination, or fortune-telling. This system slowly developed into the ideographs of Chinese characters, and became an important tool for record-keeping and communication. Chinese religious ideas, especially the concept of ancestor-worship, were also developed and codified at this time.

Much of traditional Chinese philosophy emerged during the Spring and Autumn period (from the eighth to the fifth centuries BC) and the Warring States period (fifth through third centuries BC). There were so many different systems of ethics, aesthetics, government, and natural philosophy proposed by scholars at the courts of different kings that the era is also called the Hundred Schools of Thought. Much of their thought survived as written documents and gave educated Chinese in later eras a huge body of knowledge and speculations on the nature of humanity on which to draw.

Imperial Bureaucracy Emerges and Flourishes

In 221 BC, the ruler of the state of Qin was able to unify all of what was then China (a region that was less than half of China's size today) and to create a centralized state. In a radical departure from past practice, he appointed his nonhereditary representatives for fixed terms as governors of various provinces, districts, and so on. "Centralization, achieved by ruthless methods, was focused on standardizing legal codes and bureaucratic procedures, the forms of writing and coinage, and the pattern of thought and scholarship" (Shinn and Worden 1988: 11).

The Qin dynasty, led by its totalitarian ruler, Qin Shi Huangdi, only lasted 14 years, but it had a profound influence on Chinese history. All later dynasties (until the 1911 revolution) used the same pattern of government: a hereditary emperor at the head of a bureaucratic government. Emperors might come and go, often being overthrown by rivals, rebels, or invasions from outside China's borders; but the basic system of government under which the vast majority of the population lived continued for more than 2,000 years.

Scholars have profound disagreements over the amount of benefit that this system brought to ordinary people. In Wittfogel's hydraulic theory of oriental despotism (1957), the despotic ruler is able to mobilize a vast workforce to build and maintain irrigation systems on which the majority of the population rely for food production. These systems of canals also served as communication routes, especially the Grand Canal from south China to near Beijing, allowing for trade and the emergence of large urban areas and traditional industry. In this view, the villager is at least partially dependent on the government for a higher standard of living.

Many other observers, including many Chinese scholars, take a less tolerant view. They see the imperial state as providing little to farmers and chiefly being interested in exploiting them. "China's rulers have been only concerned with the maintenance of order and the collection of taxes; aside from demanding their submission, they have demanded no other cooperation from the people" (Burgess 1928: 213). They point out that aside from tax collection, villages were virtually left alone by the government. Villagers had to settle their own disputes, organize their own self-help, develop their own "crop-watching societies" to prevent their grain from being stolen, and generally try to do their best to avoid attracting the notice of a rapacious officialdom that saw them as the sheep to be sheared.

Much of the history of China is a story of alternating periods of economic progress under good governors and emperors and lean times under bad ones. Alien invasion and peasant revolts were common; some grew so large that they overthrew the emperor himself (the first Ming emperor was such a rebel, and the Yuan and Qing dynasties were established by invading non-Han emperors). Secret societies existed to protect or terrorize, depending on one's point of view and affiliation; and bandits were common in remote regions.

Yet throughout the imperial era, important technological advances were made, especially in farming. Rice-paddy agriculture was a very dependable and highly productive system of cultivation, and it slowly spread over much of south and western China. As late as 1600, the average Chinese peasant probably lived better than his or her European counterpart. One of history's great puzzles is why no Scientific Revolution, which helped spawn the Industrial Revolution, ever occurred in China. Many of the preconditions for technological progress existed in China in the early modern age; the Chinese were already responsible for the invention of gunpowder, rockets, the compass, paper, and movable type. Yet by the eighteenth century Chinese science was clearly falling behind that of Western Europe, especially in that most important of all areas, military technology.

Compared to most traditional social systems, imperial China had a relatively open system of stratification. Migration was permitted, as was occupational mobility. Entry into the imperial **bureaucracy** was through a series of examinations that tested one's knowledge of the Confucian classical texts and one's ability to write an elegant essay in classical Chinese, which was quite different from the everyday spoken language. Although usually only the middle and upper classes could afford to employ tutors to train their sons in these skills, enough stories circulated of peasants' offspring who became rich officials through the examination system that it maintained its legitimacy throughout society as a way of ranking people in the social order.

Collision with the Western Powers

By the time the European powers began to be seriously interested in China as either a place to colonize or as a trading partner (the late eighteenth century), China, like other world regions, had fallen far behind them in military prowess. The reasons are complex: an aversion to sea power and maritime trade on the part of the Manchu government (the Qing dynasty emperors), a growing population and a growing problem of tax collection, and many other difficulties.

By the mid-nineteenth century China was beset by four major revolts, including the Taiping Rebellion, which lasted for 15 years and resulted in the death of perhaps 20 million people. The colonial powers saw China as another area to expand; their attempts to carve off portions of China (the Japanese in northeast China, then called Manchuria; the Germans on the Shandong Peninsula; and the British in Hong Kong) were chiefly restrained by the jealousy of the other foreign powers, not by military or political action of the Qing dynasty.

In 1911, the Qing dynasty was finally overthrown by an unstable coalition of middle-class revolutionaries and military leaders. While Sun Yat-sen (1866–1925) proclaimed himself leader of China in the south, General Yuan Shih-kai (1859–1916) held power in the north. When Yuan died in 1916, an accelerated struggle for power throughout China ensued (Spence 1990: 287). Various local generals (warlords) took this opportunity to expand their holdings, revolutionaries tried to overthrow those in power, and foreign powers tried to add to their holdings or to enhance their trading rights in China.

During the 1920s and 1930s, two major competitors for power emerged: the Nationalist Party (the *Kuomintang*) under Chiang Kai-shek (1887–1975), and the Communist Party. They were initially allied, but after the capture of Shanghai (1927) Chiang turned on his Communist allies and massacred them throughout China's urban areas. Only a few Communist leaders were left, mostly in remote rural regions. Mao Zedong (1893–1976) emerged as an effective leader of Communist resistance to the Nationalists and discovered that China's downtrodden peasantry, rather than its industrial proletariat, could be a fertile source of revolution and revolutionaries. During the 1930s, the Communists gradually built up guerilla base areas in the countryside from which to attack the Nationalists. They developed a social technology for mobilizing peasants to turn against the chains of social custom (lease arrangements, marriage customs, and so on) that had kept them in thrall to landlords and their own relatives, especially those in powerful lineages, for hundreds of years.

While the Nationalists talked about solving China's social and economic problems, they never gained sufficient power or developed sufficient interest to take them on. Many of the officers in the Nationalist army were the sons of landlords, and they opposed any land reform programs that might benefit tenant farmers at the expense of landlords. In addition, the depredations of the Japanese imperial army in north China, culminating in the outbreak of the Sino-Japanese War in 1938 and the Japanese invasion of central and south China, led to the increasing disorganization of the Nationalist state.

At the end of this war (1938–45), the Nationalists reestablished control over most of China. Yet Nationalist officials became increasingly corrupt and inefficient. Inflation was rampant, and many areas of the nation were in ruins. The Chinese Communists, on the other hand, had been able to use their guerilla tactics against the Japanese invaders to build support among the peasantry. They moved north in 1934–36 (in the famous Long March around the western outskirts of China) to establish a base in Yenan (in Shanxi province in north China), near to Japanese-controlled areas. Although the Communist armies were not able to expel the Japanese, they treated the peasants much better than the Nationalist forces did.

During the Civil War of 1945–49, the better-equipped Nationalist army showed that it was not ready to match the political warfare of the Communists. Many poorly motivated Nationalist army units went over en masse to the Communist side. Nationalist leader Chiang Kai-shek eventually fled to Taiwan, taking with him China's air force, much of its gold reserves, and about 600,000 art objects from the Palace Museum in Beijing. The triumphant Communist Party was now ready to try to build a state structure and a classless society that could provide all Chinese with a decent standard of living and that would also be strong enough to prevent foreign aggression against China.

The late nineteenth and early twentieth century had very different effects on the social life of different strata and regions of China. In many cities, especially Shanghai, new classes of industrialists and factory workers replaced the old guild structure of urban traditional industries. The military became an important social institution and was seen as a key route of social advancement. Schools and universities emerged, and modern, largely Western, learning became an important credential, even for women.

In rural areas, there was much less **modernization.** Agricultural economists who studied north China rural life in the 1930s found that most families had only two items of foreign origin in their homes: kerosene lanterns and *yang-huo* (foreign fire, or matches). All other items of furniture, tools, clothing, and food were locally produced. Customs and social life changed more slowly, too; while the foot binding of women declined, concubinage and other forms of oppressive marriage continued. The films of Zhang Yimou (*Raise the Red Lantern; Judou*) capture some of the slow pace of change in pre-1949 China and the striking changes that took place after that date (*To Live; Farewell My Concubine*). In Chapter 3, a brief political history of the post-1949 Communist government and an examination of its effects on cultural and social change will be given.

The Population Dynamics of the World's Largest Nation

As of 1998, China is estimated to have slightly over 1.2 billion people (see Table 2–1); it is the world's most populous nation. We have only recently begun to assemble sufficient data to sketch out how China's population grew so large, why its growth has slowed dramatically, and the implications of its current population dynamics for future growth. Demographers usually focus on four key areas when they analyze population change: mortality, marriage, fertility, and migration. What follows is somewhat speculative, but is based on the best available evidence. For our purposes here, *traditional China* will refer to any time before 1949, because vital rates probably did not change dramatically, except in short-term cycles in various local areas, much before that date.

RATES OF MORTALITY, MARRIAGE, FERTILITY, AND MIGRATION IN TRADITIONAL CHINA

Mortality

Death rates in China were, as in other traditional nations, high and variable; epidemic and endemic diseases kept death rates high, as did wars and famines. Some scholars have estimated that the average **life expectancy at birth** in the first half of the twentieth century may have been in the low 20s (Barclay, Coale, Stoto and Trussell 1976), but we think this estimate is probably too low; a life expectancy in the low 30s was probably the norm in most areas. Although the question is complex, it seems impossible for China to have reached a population of about 575 million by 1952 with the kind of high death rates that would be needed to generate a life expectancy in the low 20s.

Modern Western medicine gradually filtered into China in the late nineteenth and early twentieth century, but it had little large-scale effect, especially in rural areas. Throughout the late nineteenth and early part of the twentieth century, little progress was made in immunization of

TABLE 2-1

Population Size and Birth, Death, and Growth Rates
of the People's Republic of China

Year	Population (in millions)	Crude Birth Rate (per 1,000)	Crude Death Rate (per 1,000)	Rate of Natural Increase (%)
1952	574.8	37	17	2.0
1957	646.5	34	11	2.3
1962	673.0	37	10	2.7
1965	725.4	38	10	2.8
1970	829.9	33	8	2.5
1975	924.2	23	7	1.6
1980	987.1	18	6	1.2
1985	1,058.5	21	7	1.4
1990	1,143.3	21	7	1.4
1995	1,198.5	18	6	1.2

Note: The Rate of Natural Increase (RNI) is equal to the Crude Birth Rate (CBR) minus the Crude Death Rate (CDR), with one complication. While crude birth and death rates are computed per 1,000 population, the RNI is computed as per 100, or per centum. Hence China's 1952 CBR of 37 minus its CDR of 17 is an RNI of 2.0 percent (which is, of course, the same as 20 per 1,000). A nation with an RNI of 2.0 percent per year will double its population in about 35 years; one with an RNI of 1.0 percent will double in about 70 years.

Source: State Statistical Bureau 1995a: 59.

children or in the control of such prevalent diseases as tuberculosis. In cities, exploitative working conditions in factories and other work sites led to many early deaths from accidents and disease.

Marriage

Two key aspects of marriage affect the number of children women can bear: the age at which most women marry, and the proportion of women who ever marry. In traditional China, marriage was virtually universal for women. The relatively high adult **sex ratios** (perhaps 105–110 men per women) and the custom of concubinage (perhaps 1–3 women out of every 100 women were concubines) meant that often there were not enough women available for all men to marry. Many men at the bottom of society (agricultural laborers, beggars, bandits, and so on) were probably unable to marry. Men usually married women who were two to four years younger than themselves. Due to the high death rate, this difference in age also helped to offset the high sex ratio in the **marriage market.** The lack of marriage-age women may have been due to female infanticide in traditional China, but here the data are controversial and unclear.

Fertility

Chinese culture is often portrayed as one that places a huge emphasis on the fertility of women. Confucian tradition and ancestor worship generally (see Chapter 1) place great importance on the birth of at least one male heir to carry on the family name. Anthropologists have described how the status of a new wife was not secure in her husband's household until she produced a male heir and how a common reason for taking a concubine was to produce male progeny if the primary wife did not appear to be able to accomplish this task. However, almost all of the historical studies of marital fertility in traditional China show that wives were producing children at a rate far below that of married women in traditional (i.e., pre-1800) Western Europe.

Marital Fertility   In traditional China, women's mean age at marriage was about 18 years. By their late 20s, about 99 percent of all women were married. The median age at last birth was about 41 years, leaving roughly 23 years of marital fertility for the average Chinese woman. In that interval, she produced about six children, which was far below what was biologically possible.

In traditional Western Europe, women delayed marriage until their mid-20s, and even then only about 75–85 percent of all women ever married. They typically married at about age 24 and bore their last child at about age 41. During this 17-year interval, married Western European women had, on average, about 9–10 births (Flinn 1981). Their marital fertility rate was often 80–95 percent of what is thought to be biologically possible. Although fertility outside of marriage was not unknown in China (Barrett 1980), it probably did not make a major contribution to increasing birth rates.

Why Chinese women had such dramatically lower birth rates during marriage than their traditional Western European counterparts is still a mystery; suffice it to say that the easier of the possible answers (such as access to effective means of birth control) have been ruled out. Thus while the crude birth rates (i.e., all births divided by the total population size times 1,000) in traditional China and Western Europe were fairly similar, they were achieved through entirely different mechanisms—in China by virtually universal marriage and moderate marital fertility; in Western Europe by a smaller proportion of women marrying, but with high fertility among those who did marry.

Migration

The last part of the demographic equation, migration, also functioned in a different way in China than in much of traditional Europe. In traditional Europe, with its checkerboard of tiny feudal states and estates with no centralized responsibility for resource distribution, local wars or famines could have a very severe effect. Surrounding villages, towns, or provinces had no responsibility for helping migrants trying to escape such disasters.

In China, local histories record continual wars, insurrections, crop failures, droughts, and so on; but they also record large-scale movements of populations to avoid these disasters. Local and provincial officials ran state-sponsored granaries that served local or in-migrating populations during times of crop failure. The Chinese empire was so vast that it was usually possible to escape disaster by going somewhere, even if it was only with the clothes on one's back.

The histories of many Chinese provinces show that there were successive waves of immigrants entering them and, on occasion, waves of emigrants exiting as well. Some immigrants would be escaping famines or wars, but many would trickle in, attracted by better economic conditions. Sometimes the government would sponsor large-scale immigration to develop economic opportunities (such as in the case of Yunnan province in the far south); in other cases the government might forbid migration (as in eighteenth-century Taiwan), but migration would happen anyway. Free-choice migration was probably a relatively efficient way to match up economic opportunities to population, and it may partially account for the huge rise in the traditional Chinese population relative to that of Europe before the Industrial Revolution.

POPULATION GROWTH IN THE LATE TRADITIONAL ERA

For all of the emphasis on the misery of the Chinese rural and urban populations during the late nineteenth and early twentieth century, one thing appears to be true: China's population was growing, and growing at a rate that was high by the standards of traditional populations. It has been estimated that China had about 450 million people in 1849, just before the Taiping Rebellion (1850–64), in which perhaps 20 million people perished (Ho 1959).

Many Chinese, including its first Republican leader, Sun Yat-sen, were convinced that China's population was shrinking during the early twentieth century. The heavy death toll during the conflicts of the warlord period of the 1920s, the Japanese invasion (1933–45), and the civil war between the Nationalists and the Communists (1945–49) all seem to show that China could not have seen much population increase in the first half of the twentieth century.

Yet the 1953 census, China's first modern census, showed that the nation (including Taiwan) had a population of 583 million, or at least 130 million more than the population estimated for 1900 (about 450 million). If such a large proportion of Chinese were living so close to subsistence, how could the population have grown so large? The question is still open to debate, but a number of scholars are now suggesting that even in the face of political instability in the 1910–35 era, China may have experienced a significant amount of economic growth. Unless we are willing to think that the 1953 census figures are far too high (and the 1953 data are generally confirmed by the 1964, 1982, and 1990 census data), mortality conditions in China in the first half of the twentieth century cannot have been as terrible as they are sometimes described.

SUCCESSES OF THE COMMUNIST STATE IN PUBLIC HEALTH

When the Communists took over China in 1949, they found a nation with few Western-trained doctors, no modern drug industry, few hospitals and nurses, and no system of public health. Within a few years they were able to greatly decrease the death rate by some inexpensive yet effective public health measures.

Control of Migration

As in other Communist nations of the time, the Chinese Communist Party (CCP) instituted a system of household registration and internal passport control (see Chapter 8). No one could move his or her residence without government permission, and such permission was only granted on application for specific reasons (obtaining a job in a new area, going to school elsewhere, marriage to someone of a different area, and so on). The control of population movement and the examination of those attempting to move also undoubtedly limited the spread of epidemic and endemic diseases.

Control of Deviance and Public Education

In many Chinese cities in 1949, syphilis and other venereal diseases were a major problem. By suppressing prostitution, treating infected prostitutes, and providing them alternative employment (Henriot 1995), Chinese public health authorities were able to virtually eliminate most venereal diseases. Many other diseases were attacked through educational campaigns. Many newborn infants in China died of neonatal tetanus, often because their parents practiced a custom of putting cow dung (a prime source of the tetanus bacillus) on the stump of the umbilical cord, or because the cord was cut with a contaminated tool (see Barclay 1954; Benenson 1995: 463–64). Education for parents and midwives on the dangers of these traditional customs and rudimentary sanitation helped to reduce the infant death rate.

The great increase in primary-level schooling in the 1950s (see Chapter 4) gave public health authorities another useful vehicle through which they could spread public health propaganda (wash your hands, cover food dishes between meals, don't spit everywhere) to school children and also to counter superstitious ideas about health. While the authorities often did not usually directly attack traditional principles of Chinese medicine, they made young people aware of scientific and modern approaches to health and illness.

Provision of Basic Medical Care

During the 1950s, the state began to expand basic medical services to previously uncovered groups, including people in the countryside. "Barefoot doctors," poorly trained medical personnel who could bring services to remote regions, emerged during the **Cultural Revolution** era (1966–76). Since that time, China has attempted to privatize much of its rural medical system, while maintaining some state responsibility for the maintenance of clinics and small hospitals at the township level (Liu, Liu, and Meng 1994). One important yet often-overlooked function of such a basic medical care system is that it can provide the government with knowledge of developing medical problems, such as early warning of epidemic diseases.

Mobilization for Public Health

A number of public health campaigns (see Chapter 3) in the 1950s and 1960s helped to eliminate diseases or sources of disease. For example, many villages had an open-air manure pit containing both human and animal wastes (nightsoil). While this pit was a useful source (sometimes the only source) for fertilizer, it also a vector of disease. Villages were shown how to "harden" their pits by surrounding the nightsoil with concrete and covering it so that flies and other pests could not spread disease from it. The hardening of these pits helped to safeguard supplies of drinking water.

In some cases, the intensive organization of the Chinese countryside after 1949 helped to reduce special health problems. In a number of parts of south China where rice-paddy agriculture is used, a debilitating and sometimes fatal disease called schistosomiasis is found. The disease is spread by a blood fluke that lives in humans but also in freshwater snails. During several decades after 1949, public health authorities mobilized the populations of many such regions to capture and kill snails in order to reduce the number of free-swimming blood flukes that could infect humans.

Immunization

Just as in the rest of Asia in the 1950s, China had great success in instituting childhood immunization campaigns. The immunization of children against common diseases such as rubella, polio, pertussis, diphtheria, and so on greatly reduced childhood deaths. Although the new government had few funds for bringing high-technology health care to rural dwellers, the relatively cheap provision of immunizations had a dramatic effect on the health and survival of infants and children. In addition, diseases like tuberculosis (rampant in many crowded Chinese cities) were attacked through isolation and treatment of patients. In general, the Chinese medical system throughout the past 40 years has been a relatively low-technology one, opting for the treatment of the common diseases of the many rather than the high-technology, and expensive, treatment of a few.

WHY CHINA HAS AVOIDED
MANY CHRONIC DISEASES

China has been helped in its struggle to reduce the death rate and to improve health by several factors. The Chinese rural diet, if often monotonous, is surprisingly healthy. Until the last decade or so, most Chinese farm families only ate meat or fish a few times per month, subsisting largely on starches (like rice, wheat, sweet or Irish potatoes, corn, or millet) and a variety of locally grown vegetables. Although pork is the most commonly consumed meat, it is usually consumed in such small quantities that it provides a far smaller amount of animal fat than would be true of Western diets. Chinese eat relatively little beef, a meat high in animal fat; southern Chinese eat almost no beef at all, and northerners often consume as much mutton as beef.

The traditional Chinese rural diet was low in salt, mostly because salt was expensive. The soy-sauce taste that many Americans associate with Chinese food is not found in many varieties of provincial cooking, especially rural cooking, because until recently, rural Chinese could not afford to use it. Similarly, cooking oil and meat often were in short supply (they were rationed commodities), which also decreased the amount of calories available. As a result, heart disease and diseases associated with the overconsumption of food, animal fats, or salt (such as heart disease, stroke, and diabetes) are much less common in China than in Western nations. Cerebrovascular disease (stroke), a common killer in Japan, appears to be less common in China, probably because the Chinese consume less salt.

The healthy diet was combined with ample exercise. Farm and much factory work is strenuous, and even urban dwellers often have to climb lots of stairs to get to their apartments or ride bicycles to work (Richmond 1991). Until recently, there were few overweight Chinese and lots of underweight ones. This pattern of moderate exercise even for the middle-aged and elderly also helps in avoiding ailments associated with inactivity. Many middle-aged and elderly people engage in *tai chi*, a form of exercise that gives them a moderate physical workout while also keeping them flexible.

Cancer rates vary widely throughout China. Lung cancer is a major killer in urban China. Many urban residents, especially males, smoke cigarettes; there is little effort to control smoking there. In addition, coal is often used to heat homes and offices and for fuel in factories, leading to high levels of air pollution and high rates of lung cancer for both sexes in every major industrial city in China.

For a variety of reasons, including genetic factors and a low consumption of animal fats, women in China have far lower rates of breast cancer than their counterparts in the United States or Western Europe. Colon cancer rates in China are generally lower than those in the United States, probably because the Chinese consume more fiber and less processed food than Americans. On the other hand, some cancers that are rare in the United States are common in parts of China, such as nasopharyngeal cancer, common in Guangdong province. The high incidence of hepatitis B in China, especially in southeast China, results in very high rates of liver cancer, primary hepatocellular carcinoma; in Shanghai, liver cancer is the second leading cause of cancer death, trailing only lung cancer (Editorial Committee for the Atlas of Cancer Mortality 1979).

In the near future, China will continue to have death rates higher than those of the United States, but those rates are remarkably good for a nation at its stage of economic development. Although many people are now much more able to afford better medical care, the decline in publicly funded rural health care in poorer areas since 1978 may mean that mortality and morbidity may increase in those regions. A private medical system of general practitioners, and traditional Chinese doctors and herbalists, is slowly emerging in many areas; but it appears that the state will continue to control hospitals and medical training for the near future.

By 1981, China's life expectancy at birth was reported to be 63.6 years for men and 66.3 years for women (Banister 1992b: 183). This is about the same level of life expectancy as that of white Americans in 1939–41 (Anderton et al. 1997: 145). Even though the data are not very reliable, it appears that since 1981 China's life expectancy has increased significantly. During the 1980s, Chinese demographers were predicting that the country's life expectancy (both sexes) would reach 74.6 years by the year 2025, or about one year of life expectancy less than the U.S. level in 1991 (see Cho 1992: 77); but it now appears probable that it will reach this level much sooner.

Very significant differentials in health and mortality exist between urban and rural areas and between Han and minority regions. For example, life expectancy at birth in 1981 for women in Shanghai (China's largest city) was 75.4 years, but it was only 71.6 years in Henan (a largely rural province) and 62.2 years in Guizhou (a heavily rural province with a large population of the Zhuang minority group; see Banister 1992b: 183). In the early 1980s, the Uigurs (largely in Xinjiang province), Tibetans, and the Tujia (a minority group mainly found in Hubei province) all had life expectancies around 40 years at birth (Poston and Jing 1987). Much of the difference in life expectancy across China is due to persistent differences in infant mortality (Banister 1992b).

THE PROBLEM OF POPULATION GROWTH

The decline in the death rate in China after 1949 was a mixed blessing. As Table 2–1 shows, there was a large drop in the death rate after 1949, but no major decrease in the birth rate until the early 1970s (Banister 1987). As a result, the Chinese population grew very rapidly (at about 2.5 percent per year) during the first two decades of Communist rule (Coale 1984). In absolute terms, the population of mainland China (excluding Taiwan and Hong Kong) grew by 88 million from 1950 to 1960 (from 562.6 million to 650.7 million), then grew almost 70 million more by 1970 (to 820.4 million).

The Three Bitter Years, 1959–1961

Both of these rates of growth for the decades of 1950–60 and 1960–70 are depressed by the largest famine in world history, or what the Chinese call the **Three Bitter Years** of 1959–61. This famine occurred after the failure of the ambitious and ill-conceived **Great Leap Forward** of 1958 (see Chapter 3). Demographers estimate that between 30 and 35 million extra people (i.e., over and above normal death rates) died in this three-year period (Ashton, Hill, Piazza, and Zeitz 1984). Because of government secrecy and the concentration of loss of life among rural dwellers, the extent of this huge loss of life in this largely man-made catastrophe has attracted little attention among Chinese or foreigners.

The Great Leap Forward (1958–60) was the attempt by Chinese leader Mao Zedong (or Mao Tse-tung) to boost China's agricultural and industrial production. During this campaign, large numbers of farmers were taken away from planting and harvesting food crops and put to work building dams or backyard steel furnaces that usually produced worthless products. As a result, food production dipped to dangerous levels: "The average amount of grain that had been available to each person in China's countryside, which had been 205 kilos in 1957 and 201 kilos in 1958, dropped to a disastrous 183 kilos in 1959, and a catastrophic 156 kilos in 1960. In 1961 it fell again—to 134 kilos" (Spence 1990: 583).

In famines, it is the very old and the very young who suffer most. Although we will probably never know the true extent of suffering in rural China at that time, an examination of the size of birth cohorts who survived to age 25–35 in the 1990 census (i.e., born between July 1954 and June 1965) will give some idea of the number of babies who were either never born or who died soon after birth due to the famine. The number of those age 32 in 1990 (born July 1957–June 1958) was 19.06 million, just before the famine hit. The number born between July 1958–June 1959 (the first peak of the famine, those age 31 in 1990) dropped to 14.38 million, a decline of almost one-quarter (24.6 percent) compared to the prior year's births (or survivors). The second wave of the famine hit in 1960, causing those born between July 1960–June 1960 (age 29 in 1990) to drop to 11.50 million, or 7.56 million people fewer than the size of the 32-year-old birth cohort (Population Census Office 1993b: 3).

Spence puts it a slightly different way: "In the China of 1957, before the Great Leap began, the median age of those dying was 17.6 years; in 1963 it was down to 9.7. Half of those dying in China in that year, in other words, were under 10 years old. The Great Leap Forward, launched in the name of strengthening the nation by summoning all the people's energies, had turned back on itself and ended by devouring its young" (1990: 583). There were other, more long-term but less obvious effects of the famine: the physical stunting a generation of rural children who received insufficient protein and calories, and the widespread mental retardation of young children and infants who survived but received insufficient vitamins and nutrition. Few studies of this era exist, partially because "archives on the Great Leap Famine remain tightly guarded" since "many members of the current elite in China played a part in that inglorious era and have no interest in displaying their dirty linen" (Yang 1996: vii).

Chinese Population Dynamics
since the Three Bitter Years

The sizes of birth cohorts born after 1962 show that Chinese infant and child survivorship rates bounced back after the Three Bitter Years. By the late 1960s, Chinese birth rates were high. Even though birth control programs had been instituted in major cities, they were having little effect on the rate of population increase. The societal disorganization resulting from the Cultural Revolution and Mao Zedong's well-known anti–birth control stance also hampered population control efforts in this period.

In the early 1970s, the government instituted a campaign to raise the age at first marriage and to limit the number of births within marriage. This *wan, xi, shao* (*xi* is pronounced shee) program (later marriage, a longer interval between children, and fewer births) was instituted throughout China. In urban areas, men were told to delay marriage until age 28, and women until age 25; in rural areas, the ages were 25 and 23 years (Cho 1992: 63). Although this program was partially successful, marriage market effects (especially the increasing ratio of marriageable men to women in the late 1970s) undercut efforts to raise the marriage age of women.

As a result of government concern over how rapidly the population was growing, a **One-Child Policy** was instituted in 1979. This policy limited all Chinese couples (except for national minorities) to a single child (regardless of sex) and relied on a mix of persuasion and coercion to force couples to use contraception effectively and to abort any fetuses not in the government birth plan. Parents who had unapproved children could suffer financial penalties, castigation by political leaders, or even have their houses pulled down.

The campaign to control fertility was much more successful than the effort to raise the marriage age. Between 1972 and 1981 the Crude Birth Rate dropped 40.3 percent, from 34.5 births per 1,000 people to 20.6 per 1,000 people (Cho 1992: 71). While this level of fertility is still above what would be necessary for a true one-child policy, it is still a remarkable achievement for an underdeveloped nation in such a short period of time.

China has maintained this level of low fertility throughout the 1980s (Poston 1992). Limited data from the 1990s indicate that while there may have been a slight rise in fertility in rural areas in the 1990s, the aging of the population (also due to the One-Child Policy) in recent years has resulted in fewer women in the child-bearing years. One key question is whether the decline in fertility is sufficiently institutionalized in the countryside that the birth rate would stay low even if the strong government pressure to limit fertility was removed (Chapter 6).

This huge decline in fertility was not attained without cost. There is little doubt that a large number of women were forced to have abortions against their will. The high sex ratios among infants and children

The Zhang (pronounced Jahng) family in 1970, shortly before urban family planning policies began. Note the large proportion of young people and children, and the uniformity and virtually unisex nature of Cultural Revolution dress.

indicate that sex-selective infanticide and abortion are prevalent in some areas of rural China, especially for women's second and third pregnancies. On the other hand, the improvements in life (in terms of material progress, human rights and other areas) during the past two decades would probably have been delayed if not made impossible if China had continued to have such a high birth rate. There is now some evidence that the government is moving away from punitive measures to prevent extra births and towards the measures used in many other Third World population planning programs (sex and maternal education, better provision of inexpensive contraceptives, and so on) to reduce births in rural areas (*Chicago Tribune* May 24, 1998: A-1).

Almost all migration within China between 1949 and 1978 was government-sponsored, usually for reasons of economic development or national defense. After 1978, the government began to allow some free migration, a practice that had been virtually forbidden (especially for rural residents) after 1949 (see Chapters 8 and 9). Over the last decade, there has been a vast surge in migration in China, both from rural areas to urban ones (often in southeast China) and more recently between rural areas. Most of these migrants are motivated by economics: They feel that they can make more money elsewhere. There is only a limited amount of overseas migration of graduate students (mostly to the United States) and migration of Chinese labor to overseas jobs; there were estimated to be fewer than 400,000 such workers in 1996

(*Far Eastern Economic Review* May 29, 1997: 50). Migration into China is of almost no consequence. Thus while migration is of importance in re-distributing China's population, especially now that the birth rate has declined, China is largely outside of the vast streams of workers and refugees flowing between many nations.

SUMMARY

During the second half of the twentieth century, China saw a rapid drop in the death rate, followed by an even more rapid drop in the birth rate between about 1970 and the early 1980s. Compared to other countries, China's life expectancy is fairly high relative to its level of per-person income; and this will probably continue to improve at a better-than-average rate in the future as well.

Although marriage age has increased slightly, almost all Chinese women, and a somewhat smaller proportion of all Chinese men, will eventually marry. Migration, a common phenomenon before 1949, has become an important factor in Chinese population dynamics after a three-decade hiatus (1949–78) when most of the population was virtually immobile. China's growth rate will probably continue to slow in the early decades of the next century, and India (which has no One-Child Policy) will surpass China as the world's most populous nation within the next three decades.

CHAPTER 3

Politics Takes Command: Effects on Social Structure and Culture

Every nation's political system is formed by historical forces and current problems. American political leaders and jurists try to ransack the Constitution to try to figure out what Jefferson, Madison, or Hamilton might have thought about what can or cannot be sent over the Internet, as if such a system of communication was even imaginable to leaders who measured communication by the speed of a horse (Ambrose 1997: 52–54). Chinese leaders today face much the same problem: They have a political system designed to meet the problems of the 1940s and 1950s (national survival in a hostile world, suppression of internal enemies, redistribution of rural wealth in a more equitable way) in an environment that has changed a great deal.

This chapter will examine some of the forces and events that have affected China's political organization and their effects on Chinese society. More than in almost any other nation, examining political organization in China is a key to understanding social organization because the state *demanded* that individuals conform to the larger political goals of the state. It also developed an elaborate technology for compelling compliance and for discovering and punishing noncompliance. This technology had its roots in both Confucian traditions and methods and in an imported Leninist form of government (i.e., the Soviet-style Communist system). Since most of those aged 40 and older in China today (who wield most of the power) grew up under this system, understanding how it functioned will give some insight into how their views of social roles, behavior, and structure were formed.

A BRIEF TIME LINE OF THE PEOPLE'S REPUBLIC

After Communist forces ejected the *Kuomintang* (Nationalist Chinese) government from all of China except Taiwan, Mao Zedong proclaimed the establishment of the People's Republic of China on October 1, 1949; this date is now commemorated as China's National Day. From 1950 to

1953, the Communist Party consolidated its hold on power in rural areas by conducting the **Land Reform Campaign,** which confiscated land from landlords, rich peasants, and sometimes "middle peasants" and distributed it to poor and landless farmers (see Table 3–1).

In late 1950, China entered the Korean War on the North Korean side, opposing the United Nations (mainly U.S.) armed forces. The need for a wartime mobilization and the presence of a powerful external enemy gave fresh impetus to the Communist Party's attempts to control industry and urban life as well. The party launched a series of mass movements in urban areas, including a campaign to seek out counterrevolutionaries (1951–53), a movement against corruption among cadres (the Three-Anti Campaign, 1951–52), and finally a campaign to take over industrial enterprises from the bourgeoisie (the Five-Anti Campaign of 1951–52; see Teiwes 1997: 37–40). In addition, various campaigns to reeducate the population against "superstition," especially against Christianity, were carried out in different regions of China to make sure that there were no surviving rivals to Communist orthodoxy.

In 1953, the first large-scale attempt at centralized government planning, the Transition to Socialism, was instituted. This Stalinist-style five-year plan set goals of production and consumption for different industries and for the agricultural sector. Collectivization of agriculture (combining farmers into joint work units with joint responsibility for production and consumption) began. Mutual aid teams, the forerunners of production teams (see Chapter 7), were formed out of groups of 10–30 households in many areas of China in the early 1950s. By the mid-1950s, the Communist Party encouraged the development of larger agricultural units called Agricultural Producers' Cooperatives. In these units, farmers shared resources (such as draft animals and the little available agricultural machinery), work responsibilities, and the product of their labor with all other farmers in the village. Farmers were given work points for each hour of labor, and at the end of the year the unit's harvest would be divided among farm households according to how many work points the members of each household had earned.

Mao and other Communist Party leaders became convinced that the Agricultural Producers' Cooperatives were a great success and could lead the way to even greater breakthroughs in agriculture if they could be combined into larger-scale agricultural units, the People's Communes. The Great Leap Forward of 1958 was an attempt to make breakthroughs in both agriculture and industry. As was shown in Chapter 2, it had disastrous consequences during 1959–61. The Communist Party had to retreat on a number of fronts; its fervent belief that ideology could overcome technical obstacles had been shown to be false, and many Chinese (especially those in rural areas) had become cynical about such political mobilization. In addition, after the Hundred Flowers period and the Anti-Rightist Campaign, many Chinese had learned how dangerous it could be to express one's true opinion, even in one's own home, rather than mouthing stock propaganda phrases.

TABLE 3-1

Chronology of Major Events in China since the Communist Revolution

Time Period	Event
1945–49	Civil war between Nationalist (Kuomintang) and Communist Party armies.
1949	Communists victorious in China; Mao Zedong proclaims founding of the People's Republic; Nationalists flee to Taiwan, establish regime there.
1950–53	China fights in Korean War against United Nations forces.
1950–53	Land Reform Campaigns in different parts of rural China to redistribute land from landlords to tenant farmers.
Early 1950s	Campaigns in urban areas to socialize major industries and against corruption, the bourgeoisie, and Christianity.
1953–57	Transition to Socialism; first five-year plan; collectivization of agriculture.
1957	Anti-Rightist Campaign; aimed at intellectuals.
1958–60	Great Leap Forward; attempt to increase production.
1959–61	Three Bitter Years; period of massive starvation in the countryside.
1962–65	Period of economic recovery.
1966–68	Cultural Revolution; most radical phase.
1969–71	Rise of Jiang Qing (Mao Zedong's wife) and the Gang of Four.
1972	President Richard Nixon visits China.
1972–76	Period of more moderate political and economic policies.
1976	Death of Mao Zedong and Zhou Enlai; radicals remove Deng Xiaoping from government; Hua Guofeng leads China.
1978	Deng Xiaoping replaces Hua Guofeng as China's leader; Four Modernizations campaign (to help China catch up in agriculture, industry, science, and national defense) instituted.
1979	Democracy Wall; early post-Mao attempt at democratic expression via big-character posters put up on a wall in Beijing.
1979–98	Growth of nonsocialist economy in China; "responsibility system" (return to family farming) in countryside, growth of private firms.
1989	Tiananmen demonstrations; students and others demand democratic rule, but are suppressed in June 1989.
1992	Deng Xiaoping tours south China and gives his blessing to economic reforms; economy goes into high gear.
1997	Deng Xiaoping dies; Jiang Zimin is president and Communist Party secretary. Hong Kong changes from being a British Crown Colony to a Special Administrative Area of the People's Republic of China.

During the early 1960s, a group of less ideological, more pragmatic leaders (including Deng Xiaoping, 1904–97) began to control policy in China. They reorganized agriculture into smaller, more manageable administrative units and emphasized technical achievement over political purity in industry. Production in agriculture and industry slowly recovered. The leadership also tried to reestablish discipline within the Communist Party by prosecuting corrupt cadres through the Socialist Education Campaign in the early 1960s (Lieberthal 1997: 136–38).

By the mid-1960s, Mao was increasingly concerned that his idealized vision of China was fading, and China was being increasingly ruled by an officialdom that exhibited the worst characteristics of both modern Communist and traditional Chinese bureaucracies (Whyte 1973). The Proletarian Cultural Revolution was Mao's attempt to regain power by overthrowing these officials. In order to do so, Mao tried an end run around the Communist Party by appealing directly to students, the military, and other groups who could help him overthrow its bureaucratic apparatus and restore ideological purity to the nation.

The Cultural Revolution, especially its most radical phase (1966–68), threw Chinese schools and cities into turmoil. During 1967–69, the People's Liberation Army took power in many Chinese cities and smashed the power of the student groups (the Red Guards), who had frequently become little more than warlord groups squabbling over power. While China became less isolated on the international front (President Richard Nixon visited China in 1972), Chinese urban administration and industry gradually recovered (the agricultural sector had been scarcely touched by the uproar).

As Mao aged and his health declined, the **Gang of Four,** including his wife, Jiang Qing (1914–96), controlled the nation. With the death of Mao and elder statesman Zhou Enlai in 1976, a more moderate leader, Hua Guofeng (1920–89), took over. However, Hua was a leader of little vision and was not able to govern the divided nation very effectively. By 1978, Deng Xiaoping, long opposed by the Gang of Four as a Communist Party bureaucrat, took control.

Deng placed China on an entirely new path. He recognized that the internal political turmoil and lack of economic growth had made China weak, both in terms of satisfying the needs of its citizens and in its ability to deal with other nations. He instituted the **Four Modernizations** campaign, designed to allow China to modernize in agriculture, industry, science and technology, and national defense. Political activities were to be deliberately curtailed, and the Communist Party was to have less dominance over the economy. Deng's first major accomplishment was decollectivization, or the institution of the **household responsibility system** that returned China to family farming (Chapter 9). Within a decade, rural incomes had doubled, and rural prosperity and the opening of China's economy to foreign investment and international trade ignited a surge in the private service and industrial sectors as well.

The decline in political repression in the late 1970s led to early stirrings of intellectual freedom. Some manifestations, like Beijing's 1979 Democracy Wall, used a Maoist/Cultural Revolution form of propaganda (big-character posters that usually denounced someone) to ask for an end to political repression or demand human rights. The government was no longer as capable of keeping secrets: When it sentenced democracy advocate Wei Jingsheng (1949–) to 15 years in prison (he was finally allowed to go into exile in the United States in 1997), both the international press and many educated Chinese knew what had happened.

Over the past two decades, the Communist Party has been trying to ride the tiger of rapid economic development without ending up inside. Sometimes foreign influences are encouraged, and sometimes (as in the 1983 campaign against "spiritual pollution," or Western thought) they are presented as dangerous trends. By the late 1980s, demands for democracy and denunciations of corruption among Communist Party officials were widespread.

In the spring of 1989, a student-led movement in several major cities led to demonstrations against the Communist Party (Calhoun 1995). The students took over **Tiananmen Square,** which had roughly the same symbolic value as if an American student group had taken over the Mall in Washington, DC. During that spring it has been estimated that about one million Beijing residents marched in support of the students' reform demands.

Within the beleaguered Communist Party, the hard-liners gradually gained control. On June 3–4, 1989, they sent special army units (from rural posts far outside Beijing) in to break up the demonstrations. As they came down Changan Jie (a major east-west boulevard into Tiananmen Square) in tanks and armored personnel carriers, guns blazing, hundreds of students and ordinary citizens were killed (Spence 1990: 743). The Party had reasserted itself, and the "Democracy Spring" of 1989 in Beijing and other Chinese cities was over.

Yet when the Communist Party and the security apparatus tried to capture the leaders of the student movement, they often seemed curiously inept. China after 1989 was still a Communist state, but there were many other foreign and non-Communist domestic influences on the population (see Chapter 8). Perhaps one of the most important long-term influences of this era has been the distrust by the leadership of higher education and its lack of support for it (see Chapter 4), which will have major effects on human resource availability in China in the future.

THE LEGACY OF REVOLUTION

Many of the policies that the Communist Party used in governing China from 1949 through the present are derived from what it perceived as successful strategies in its revolutionary struggle. These strategies include methods of controlling and motivating the population (the people), isolating opponents (class enemies), and ensuring conformity among its own members and supporters (cadres and activists).

The rapid growth of the Communist Party and its ability to take over large areas of rural north China between about 1937 and 1945 was due to its appeal to the peasantry on the dimensions of social reform and nationalism. These farmers had suffered under the depredations of both landlords and the Japanese invaders and responded positively to the Communists' appeals for social justice and patriotic opposition to Japanese oppression.

During this period a uniquely Chinese form of Marxism, which is usually called **Maoism,** emerged. Communist leaders, called **cadres,** were supposed to keep in close touch with the peasantry, learning about local issues and concerns. They were supposed to inform the central leadership about these matters, but once the leadership made policy decisions, these local cadres were to carry out the policy in a wholehearted manner. This process of information flowing upward in the organization and policy flowing down was called *democratic centralism,* a characteristic of many Communist states.

In China, however, certain social-ecological constraints (Chapter 1) on the administration of the Communist Party made the leadership emphasize the human side of the process. China is a vast nation, with a wide variety of local conditions. Before 1949, Communist leaders were often guerilla chiefs in isolated hill regions with whom it was hard for the leadership to keep in contact. It was almost impossible to develop a set of rules that would fit every situation. Instead, the party had to depend on the ability of the local leadership to understand local conditions and to apply general rules in a sensible way.

Thus the allegiance of the local leadership (the cadres) became of paramount importance. In imperial China (before 1911), the emperor tried to ensure good administration by appointing those imbued with the norms and values of Confucianism. Unable to control and oversee all its local administrators, the Communist Party stressed ideological training and slowly began to supplement training in Marxism-Leninism (an approach used in the Soviet Union) with the study of Mao Zedong thought.

To the Communist Party, there were two principal problems that had to be addressed. There were some party members who were not sufficiently revolutionary, who wanted to make compromises with feudal elements, the **bourgeoisie,** and so on. There were also those who had their own interpretations of Marxist thought, those who might disagree with Mao on points of theory or who disagreed with how party policy was to be applied. These hidden "deviationists" were even more dangerous, because they might hijack the party apparatus and substitute some other ideology for the thought of Mao Zedong.

The Chinese Communists, like their Confucian forebears, saw the problem of successful revolution not mainly in terms of the number of guns or soldiers, but rather in whether there were a sufficient number of revolutionary cadres of "virtue and ability" (in the Marxist sense) to allow the party to triumph (Schurmann 1968: 164). This meant that the ideological training of party cadres, and later the population at large, would be of fundamental importance. By the time of the Cultural Revolution (1966–68), the Maoist leadership wanted the entire nation to be, as they termed it, "one big school of Mao Zedong thought." Even after this attempt to motivate the entire country to follow one man's thought, the Communist Party's emphasis on ideological education and conformity would continue until the present.

CONTROLLING AND MOTIVATING THE POPULATION

The first problem that the Communist cadres faced in the countryside was that most farmers were apolitical; they were far more interested in survival and perhaps putting away a little money than in engaging in the risky business of opposing the governing authorities. Here, the Communists were greatly aided by the rapacious nature of Chinese warlord and Japanese puppet governments; by the time they arrived, the peasantry had often already been stripped of the possessions that it might have been afraid to risk. Any social contract between the peasantry and the government authorities or the rural upper classes was also almost nonexistent, so that traditional rural social bonds did not stand in the way of revolutionary mobilization.

The Chinese Communists became very adept at analyzing the grievances of local peasants, especially those of the poorest classes, and setting one social class against another. They also used a variety of propaganda techniques to motivate these largely illiterate peasants: songs, posters, plays, and so on. In the short term, the Communists wanted to deny rural produce and manpower to their political class enemies, but they had broader goals as well:

> They wanted not only to end class exploitation and landlessness but to produce an egalitarian society in which individuals would work for the common good rather than to advance the interests of their own family, a society in which power would rest on devotion to national goals rather than on loyalty to particular kinship groups, and in which freeing of peasants from the bonds of feudal customs and superstitions would release boundless human energies for the building of a more abundant society. (Parish and Whyte 1978: 8)

The Communists became adept at spotting potential leaders in villages: men and women who seemed to be swayed by the new revolutionary movement, who were willing to take risks to support it, and who could influence others. These **activists** would be used to encourage group activities to support the revolution, to spot spies or traitors, and to carry the revolutionary message in surrounding villages because they could speak the local dialect. Some of these activists would eventually be offered membership in the Youth League and finally in the Communist Party.

After 1949, these same techniques were continued in rural areas, especially during the Land Reform Campaign (1950–53). Peasants became even more interested, because now there was something concrete to be gained from participation (the land, animals, and furniture of landlords and rich peasants) at relatively little risk. Yet in many villages, the internal conflicts within families, and even within individuals themselves, grew greater as they had to attack feudal institutions in which they had participated, such as the lineage hall or the village temple, or to denounce individuals whom they knew personally, such as rich relatives or a friend who was a former low-level government official (Yang 1965).

Before 1949, the Communist Party was never very successful in controlling urban areas; its penetration was mostly limited to spies and sympathizers. Surprisingly, for a party of the working class, it made little attempt after the 1927 massacre of its cadres and supporters (Chapter 1) to rebuild a strong base of support there. As a result, when the party took over Chinese cities, most of its initial system of control was similar to that of other Communist states: tight control through a household registration system (see Chapter 8) and a strong police presence. It was not until it gained control of workplaces and schools that the urban system of control and motivation took on its distinctive Maoist features: activists, campaigns, and so on.

Ensuring Conformity

For many Western social scientists in the 1950s and 1960s, the most distinctive part of the Maoist apparatus of political control, and the one with the most implications for social and cultural change, was **thought reform** (*sixiang gaizao*, pronounced sis-syang-guy-zao; see Schurmann, 1968: 45–50; Lifton 1969).

Developed from methods used by Communist Party cells before 1949 and in the former Soviet Union, thought reform involved the "moral and psychological transformation of the individual" (Schurmann 1968: 45–46). Party members or other individuals who were suspected of wrongdoing had to write and rewrite their autobiographies, which were then checked against dossiers of information (*dangan*, pronounced dahng-ahn) that the Communist Party held on them.

The subject of thought reform was then subjected to a grueling series of interviews with a group of other people who criticized this person's behavior, probing for inconsistencies, lies, or self-serving statements. This criticism was conducted from the standpoint of Maoist thought, attacking the subject through using its categories of social class, error, historical analysis, and so on. The subject was then required to write a new self-criticism, recognizing past faults and flaws and demonstrating that through a better understanding of Maoism such actions would be avoided in the future. This process could go on numerous times; in many cases, finding that his or her self-criticism documents were rejected by the group, the subject of thought reform had to think up new crimes or sins to confess.

Part of the supposed sincerity of this self-criticism was measured by the individual's willingness to implicate others and to provide information that could be used against them (Cheng 1986: 277–300). Throughout the process, the subject never knew what the final outcome would be; the interrogators would stress that the degree of punishment would be related more to the sincerity of the confession than to the gravity of the crimes. The use of thought reform spread to schools, prisons, workplaces, and other settings (Whyte 1972). It was generally most effective in changing individual behavior in **total institutions,** that is, in social institutions where all aspects of the individual's life could be controlled.

Some aspects of thought reform are similar to Western psychological techniques used for behavior change in individuals, such as group therapy (Schurmann 1968: 48). Yet in some ways it is linked to Chinese cultural values. For example, child socialization in China leads most individuals to place a higher value on group conformity (see Chapter 4). Verbal, and sometimes even physical, attacks by group members probably have a more profound effect on Chinese than on more individualistic Americans. Public humiliation in a society where "face" is considered important could be devastating. Much of what is done in thought reform would be seen by Americans as an attack on the private life of the individual. Yet in traditional China, the concepts of individualism or privacy never really existed, and in Maoist China they became culpable acts.

Campaigns

One method used extensively by the Communist Party in its efforts to create social change was the campaign. **Campaigns** were recurring broad-based movements with a particular end in mind: land reform, suppressing the bourgeoisie, finding enemies of Chairman Mao, getting rid of insect pests. They usually involved labor over and above that normally required from the population; people might be required to contribute extra hours of work or to attend meetings at which local leaders and activists would explain the purpose of the campaign and attempt to whip up enthusiasm for it.

Campaigns also served what sociologists call **latent functions** for the regime. They could get more work out of the population without the necessity of giving them more pay. During a campaign, new activists might come to the fore and be identified for possible future leadership positions. Those who did not participate, or only participated in a nominal way, could also be identified, and this might be recorded in their political record.

Sometimes, campaigns could take unexpected twists and turns. During the early 1950s, it appeared that much of the emphasis in thought reform was to convert those who had grown up under the old capitalist system. By the mid-1950s, many Communists thought that most of the population was happy with the new regime. In 1957, Mao invited the Chinese people, especially the intellectuals, to tell the Communist Party how it might reform itself and do a better job of modernizing China: "Let a hundred flowers bloom, let a thousand schools [of thought] contend." Yet the volume, depth, and intensity of the widespread criticism of the party that emerged from this Hundred Flowers period shocked party leaders, and soon afterward (1957) they launched the Anti-Rightist Campaign to seek out those who dared criticize the leadership of the new China. Within a few months, over a half-million people were denounced and punished as rightists, and tens of thousands would die in prison camps (Kristof and WuDunn 1994: 66).

The **ideal type** of the classic Maoist political campaign was the Cultural Revolution. This campaign was Mao's device to reassert his control against party bureaucrats by using students and other groups to "bombard the center" by forming Red Guard detachments and attacking the political authorities. Beginning in schools, these Red Guards, who had pledged their loyalty to Chairman Mao, began to search for and find "class enemies" among their teachers and administrators. They quickly moved on to attacking the Communist Party headquarters in many cities and virtually paralyzed urban government between 1966 and 1968.

As well as a political movement, the Cultural Revolution was a large-scale attack on the traditional culture of China. Huge numbers of books, paintings, sculptures, and pieces of pottery were destroyed (Cheng 1986); many Buddhist and Daoist temples were looted and torn down. People found with Western classical music in their homes were accused of "worshiping foreign things."

The Cultural Revolution also attempted to change the process of status attainment in China. Universities were closed down because they were too elitist, and various forms of practical training ("Students must learn from peasants and workers!") were instituted instead. One no longer took examinations to qualify for advanced training; instead, the political authorities in one's work unit recommended those with the best class background (usually the class status of one's parents at the time of the 1949 revolution) and the best class attitude for future advancement.

The Cultural Revolution is also an example of the final stage of Maoism: the attempt to achieve a "permanent revolution." Mao and his followers attacked the new groups that were emerging in China—Communist bureaucrats, intellectuals, technicians, and so on—as groups that could and would undermine the purity of the peasants' and workers' state. Mao's attempt to cleanse China of foreign influence and to build an educational system where political orthodoxy was more important than performance in the classroom or on the job (the preference for "Reds" rather than experts) cost China two decades of economic growth.

Models

In a vast and largely uneducated nation, the Communist Party found that it was difficult to motivate people through Marxist, or Maoist, ideology alone. People, especially children, needed more concrete images or examples of good and bad behavior. Thus the press and radio (there were loudspeakers in many villages) began to tout **models,** either individuals or units, that were doing an excellent job of carrying out the goals of communism in general and the latest campaign in particular.

Probably the most famous model individual was Lei Feng, a soldier who supposedly kept a diary of his good deeds until his accidental death in the early 1960s. After his death, his diary was "found" and publicized throughout China. This model soldier, of poor peasant origin, was always careful and never wasteful of state property, understood class struggle, stayed up late to wash his comrades' socks, and so on. Students throughout China in the early 1960s were exhorted on a daily basis to be "little Lei Fengs," and competitions were held to see who could do the most socialist-style good deeds. As the goals of political and social campaigns changed over the months, new pages of Lei Feng's diary were "found" that showed that he had excellent behavior in these areas, too.

After the economic reform (1978), as the Communist Party worried that Chinese youth was becoming too materialistic and falling under the spell of Western spiritual pollution, Lei Feng was brought back as a model to emulate. In addition, more technocratic models (scientists, mathematicians, and teachers) were also held up as examples to youth. Lei Feng was dredged up again in 1989 after the army slaughtered students and workers in Tiananmen Square; he even returned in a slightly altered form in 1996 in the propaganda film *My Time after Lei Feng*. In 1996, he was joined by two new living models of socialist good behavior: Li Shuli, an overachieving ticket collector for a Beijing bus company who studied English at night, and Xu Hu (pronounced shoe who), a Shanghai plumber who worked far into the night unclogging his neighbors' pipes (*Far Eastern Economic Review* April 17, 1997: 30–31).

Another problem the party faced was that it was often difficult for those in work units to visualize how the abstract aims of campaigns applied to them. Did "walking on two legs" (meaning emphasizing both agriculture and industry) mean that they should finish building the irrigation canal or use the cement to build a small factory? A key part of many of the economic campaigns was publicizing model units that had found concrete ways of attaining the goals of the campaign. Their methods were discussed in the press, and for a time, their leaders became almost like celebrities throughout China.

The most famous model unit was Dazhai, a small, impoverished commune in the hills of Shanxi province. During the Cultural Revolution, when the Communist Party wanted to emphasize local self-reliance, it publicized how the peasants of Dazhai had used local materials, lots of hard work, and the application of Mao Zedong thought to solve their production problems and win their war against nature. The commune's leader, a peasant named Chen Yonggui, became a national hero, and hundreds of thousands of students, workers, and peasants were shipped to this remote spot so that they could learn from Dazhai.

Of course, every nation uses models; one of the authors recently discovered that his daughters' middle school had been made a "Model Middle School" by the U.S. Department of Education. The difference here was the extent to which the Chinese used them during the Maoist era (1949–76): They were integrated into the school curriculum and into the mandatory political self-study classes in offices and factories, and they appeared on billboards and were heard over loudspeakers. Living in China in those years was a bit like living in a U.S. city in the last week before a hotly contested and publicized election, except that there was only one party running.

THE END OF MAOISM

By the time of Mao's death in 1976 there was a vast lethargy in the Chinese political system. Hundreds of thousands of people, perhaps more than a million, had been killed or were forced to commit suicide, and millions of people were disgraced, or in internal exile, for what increasingly looked like trumped-up or minor charges. By 1978, the Gang of Four, Mao's key supporters in the latter stages of the Cultural Revolution, were on trial.

After the Cultural Revolution, the whole oppressive edifice did not come crashing down at once; rather, it slowly eroded. An urban sent-down youth does a good job as a work-point recorder in a distant rural production brigade, and his peasant workmates recommend that this talented fellow be sent to a university for more training. A former factory administrator, working now as a janitor, gets his job back because everyone knows he's the right person for the job, regardless of his supposed "crimes." A teacher finds one of his students reading a traditional Chinese novel, forbidden during the Cultural Revolution, but lets him go because he is impressed at how fluently the student can read the old-style Chinese characters. The return to normalcy after the Cultural Revolution was not a big battle that was won by the opponents of the Gang of Four; rather, it was a number of very small skirmishes, with people deciding that it was inhumane to apply the letter of the law.

From 1949 on, the concept of **class label** (*chengfen,* pronounced chung-fun) was of major importance in the revolutionary system of social stratification. Whether one was of worker, landlord, poor peasant, or other background became of crucial importance to one's **social mobility.** It was a truly ascriptive label: Many former landlords' children born after 1950 grew up as among the poorest, and most discriminated against, children in the village, but they still had no chance at higher education, marriage to someone of "good class background," and so on. During the 1970s, the importance of these class labels (and they were very important during the Cultural Revolution) began to fade. One possible reason for their disappearance is that so many ordinary people were given negative political labels that they saw how unfair the system was. After 1979, the class label was abandoned as a sorting mechanism for education, employment, and marriage, and the Communist Party officially referred to the 1966–76 era as the Ten Years of Catastrophe.

One other consequence of the depoliticization of Chinese society was the renewed importance of informal social networks, or *guanxi* (pronounced gwan-shee). Connections between friends, neighbors, old classmates, and others had always been important sources of information and access to resources, but in the whirlwind of entrepreneurship and development after 1979, they often became key conduits for success. These extralegal, and sometimes illegal, exchanges of introductions, favors, insider information, and preference are very prevalent in China and are responsible for a great deal of the government corruption there. In a society with few rules or laws about the proper relationships between government and business, or even any system of commercial law, these networks of personal influence and information have remained essential tools for getting things done.

One of the key underpinnings of the system of social control since 1949 has been a large-scale prison system. While such prisons are found throughout China, many are in remote regions where few Han Chinese would voluntarily want to move. The system is supposedly aimed at reform through labor, using many of the techniques for behavior change described above. The Chinese government is, along with the United States, one of the last few major nations that uses capital punishment, and like the United States, it uses prison labor to produce goods and services consumed by the world outside of the prison.

While the American press emphasizes the imprisonment of those Chinese who have engaged in political dissent, they make up only a small fraction of the imprisoned population in China. Two far larger groups are ordinary criminals or those who are imprisoned for "economic crimes," which usually involve trying to subvert the economic system for one's own personal gain. Since 1978, the rules surrounding such economic crimes have been murky and ever-changing. Large numbers of people have been convicted of, and sometimes executed for, activities that suddenly became illegal in the midst of a political campaign against one or another form of supposed corruption. The lack of written law, guarantees of individual rights, or consistent sentencing guidelines over time mean that ordinary Chinese can sometimes be sentenced to long prison terms for relatively minor offenses.

Social Orientation and Terms of Address

Much can be learned about a society from how people, both acquaintances and strangers, are addressed. In pre-1949 China, family members were sometimes addressed by their same-sex birth-order number (*lao san*, pronounced lao-sahn, "brother number three"), and wives were referred to (by themselves and others) as "so-and-so's wife," without any personal name. By the twentieth century, *xiansheng* (pronounced shian-shung) and *taitai,* (pronounced tie-tie), the rough equivalents of mister and missus, were in common use.

The communist movement tried to emphasize the equality of all by calling everyone *tongzhi,* (pronounced tohng-jir), "comrade." If a woman's marital status had to be specified, she was called an *airen,* (pronounced aye-rehn), which previously had meant something close to "lover." The term *comrade* now was supposed to be used for friends, acquaintances, and even those whom one had never met before: "Comrade, what time is the Number 27 bus supposed to get here?" The point was that in a revolutionary society, all should be treated equally (no more special treatment for friends and family) and all were engaged in a great revolutionary enterprise.

The term *comrade* was so overused during the Cultural Revolution that by the early 1980s it had fallen into disuse. Politically neutral terms like *old Yang* or *young Wang* were used between friends, acquaintances, and coworkers; the use of first names as terms of address is, unlike in the United States, still surprisingly infrequent. The pre-1949 forms of Mr. and Mrs. (*xiansheng* and *taitai*) are now often used by Chinese as a normal form of address. In an interesting twist of fate, the term *comrade* (*tongzhi*) is now used in Taiwan and Hong Kong, but by gay males to denote someone of their sexual orientation.

Reform-Era Politics

After many decades of political struggle and after the suppression of the democracy movement on June 4, 1989, most young people are not enthusiastic about getting involved in politics, either inside or outside the Communist Party. China is now mostly remarkable for its *lack* of political slogans on walls or sides of buildings; about all one sees are commercial advertisements. In a sense, China of the 1990s is a demobilized society, granting political power to the Communist Party because it is too busy elsewhere, usually making money. The Communist Party's major appeal and its chief claim to legitimacy is that it seems to be the only institution that can hold China together. It is a kind of technocratic appeal (and most of the coming generation of leaders are technocrats, not revolutionaries), and not one that excites most people.

Elements of prerevolutionary culture have also reasserted themselves. One can hear concerts of traditional Chinese music at tea houses in Beijing. In Shanghai, there is a newspaper written in pre-1949 nonsimplified characters (*fan-ti zi*, pronounced fahn-tee-dz) that was supposed to be published for the convenience of Taiwan and Hong Kong (two places where they still used *fan-ti zi*) travelers. It has become stylish for local Shanghainese to read this paper as well; being able to read *fan-ti zi* (which are still only taught in Chinese literature classes in higher schools) means that they can read pre-1949 novels, calligraphy, and other written cultural artifacts from the past 2,500 years. In the past couple of years, many Chinese have started having their names printed in *fan-ti-zi* on their name cards, apparently as a sign of their good breeding. These are not really antigovernment activities, but they certainly demonstrate a kind of individualism and a lack of fear of political persecution that was hard to find before 1978.

CHAPTER 4

Childhood and Education

Education is of great interest to sociologists because in modern societies it is not only one of the key institutions of socialization but also a major mechanism by which social stratification takes place. In a society like that of post-1949 China, where the new government was dedicated to turning the old system of stratification upside down, it was only natural that schools would become one of the major battlefields.

Yet China has also had to deal with a large number of constraints on its educational goals and policies. No matter how badly the Communist Party wanted to change the social system, it had to design mechanisms of the measurement of achievement that appeared to be fundamentally fair to most people. In addition, if it was to meet its goals of economic development, then it also needed to reward the "experts" (those who were competent technically) as well as the "reds" (those who were outstanding politically). Thus there were frequent conflicts about what should be taught, how it should be taught, who should teach it, and, most important, to whom it should be taught.

FAMILY EXPERIENCES OF CHINESE CHILDREN

The early experiences of Chinese children are not entirely dissimilar from those of American children. One major difference between Chinese and American children is that the vast majority of the former grow up in two-parent households with their natural parents present. As a result of very low rates of premarital pregnancy, low parental death rates and low divorce rates, the vast majority of Chinese children grow up with both parents overseeing and guiding them. By contrast, among children aged 5 years and younger in the United States in 1992, only about 79 percent of white children, 66 percent of Hispanic children, and 32 percent of black children were living with both parents present in the household (Anderton et al. 1997: 469-70).

Of course, the major changes in Chinese society since 1949 and over the last two decades have had profound effects on child-rearing patterns. Before 1949, the majority of rural children had mothers who were housewives (especially in the north) or who worked near the home. The mobilization of women's labor in the countryside during the 1950s for service in joint labor projects led to state support for traditional ways in which mothers could lessen the heavy burden of child care:

> They do this in several time-honored ways: adopting out or otherwise disposing of babies, especially girls, when their care would especially tax a woman who already has young children; putting children into school/day care arrangements as early as possible; turning children over to household members, including other very young children; leaving children with relatives in other households, often at a considerable distance. (Gates 1993: 268)

Chinese children usually come into frequent contact with their grandparents, particularly on their father's side. In fact, especially in rural areas, their father's parents frequently live with them, or vice versa, during some part of their upbringing, especially in their early years. Due to high rates of labor force participation among women between their 20s and 40s, children may often find that their grandparents are primary caregivers as well (Davis-Friedman 1983). Daughters-in-law in both Taiwan and mainland China seemed to have reworked the formerly very oppressive social contract between themselves and their husbands' kin: If they are expected to produce outside income for the family, then other kin (usually his parents) must contribute to child care (Ikels 1993).

Due to the impact of China's population planning programs (see Chapter 2), a child in China today has few or no siblings competing for the attention of parents, grandparents, aunts, and uncles. As any only child can tell you, this is both a curse and a blessing. In fact, in the 1980s there was a lively debate in China on whether the One-Child Policy (1979–present) has brought about a generation of "little emperors and empresses" (i.e., spoiled children) who usually get their way.

Outside the cities, the One-Child Policy really has become a one-son policy. Many Chinese rural families have two children; some have more (some Chinese demographers jokingly say that the current policy is a "one-and-a-half-child policy"). In the first half of 1990, almost half (49.4 percent) of all births in China were first births, a little under a third (31.6 percent) were second births, 12.2 percent were third births, 4.1 percent were fourth births, and 2.7 percent were fifth or higher-order births (Population Census Office, 1993a: 62). These last groups were probably heavily concentrated in national minority areas, which were less affected by family planning regulations. Aside from a greater concentration of first births, the distribution of birth orders is not strikingly different from that found in the United States in 1990, where 40.9 percent were first births, 32.1 percent were second births, 16.5 percent were third births, and 10.5 percent were fourth or higher-order births (Anderton et al. 1997: 247).

Child Rearing

In terms of actual patterns of child rearing, it is surprising to find that such a highly regimented society takes a rather relaxed view of how young children should be raised. Chinese have seldom tried to force infants and young children into rigid schedules, as was attempted by some middle-class American parents from the 1920s through the 1940s; naps, meals, and toilet-training tend to be somewhat haphazard. Partly, this is because with so many hands taking care of the child, it is hard to get everyone reading from the same page. Many Chinese remember their preschool years as a wonderful period in their life, with few rules, much attention, no responsibilities, and lots of treats.

This does not mean that children had complete freedom; parents and other older kin can and do impose their wills on children. Older children lord it over younger ones, and sons often receive preferential treatment over daughters in terms of everything from how quickly they are taken to the doctor to educational opportunities. In many places, especially in urban areas, children whose parents work attend day care at young ages and must learn to function with other children in an institutional environment.

Traditionally, in upper-class families, the relationship between mother and child was close and emotional, while that between father and child was cool and distant. This emotional distance, especially between fathers and sons, was never as common in the lower classes; from a very young age, parent and child were often coworkers, whether in the field or shop.

Passing on Values

Early childhood training reflects the values that a culture, or a social class, thinks are important to inculcate in the next generation. For the American middle class, such values as individual responsibility and competitiveness (for boys, and increasingly for girls as well) are seen as important traits to pass on. Class differences can be important as well: American working-class families tend to emphasize obedience to parents and other authority figures, whereas middle- and upper-class families may put less importance on obedience (and physical punishment) and more on self-expression, independence, and creativity.

In a society undergoing rapid social change, as in China after 1949, the transmission of values becomes much more complicated. Such values as obedience to clan elders or landlords that were appropriate in the old society obviously didn't fit post-1949 China. However, some value orientations did remain, such as that of *social exchange*. This concept, a useful one in a resource-poor, overpopulated society, is taught early in life. In traditional China, children were taught that obedience to parents and elders was rewarded. At the Chinese New Year, children would hit their foreheads on the floor in obeisance (*ke-tou*, pronounced keh-toe) to parents or other elders and receive a red envelope with money inside in return.

Traditionally, children were also taught that family members were more trustworthy than those outside of the family. Bad behavior, especially in public, was to be avoided because it shamed the family as well as the individual. Chinese children learn that their behavior, good or bad, has a broader social meaning: It can add or detract from the standing of their family and can have consequences for other family members. In addition, fights between children can escalate to conflicts between families, and this can be a very serious situation in China.

In general, the Communist state has intervened relatively little in preschool child training. It has encouraged parents to use persuasion more and corporal punishment less; in addition, it has tried to make parents and children aware that children owe obedience to the state as well as to their parents (Parish and Whyte 1978: 222). Just as in the United States, most of the values that children learn in school are not very different from those emphasized at home, and most parents appear to be satisfied with the kind of values education that their children receive (Parish and Whyte 1978: 229).

REFORMING THE OLD SCHOOL

Chinese schools have traditionally put great emphasis on rote learning, sometimes using corporal punishment, rather than trying to make learning fun or interesting. The Chinese language, with its more than 40,000 individual characters and large number of compound words (words made up of several characters), meant that learning in the lower grades involved a huge amount of memorization with little immediate use or application of the information learned. Initially incomprehensible classical Chinese texts, some of which were more than two millennia old, had to be learned exactly (*bei shu*, pronounced bay-shoe) under threat of immediate physical punishment.

During the first half of the twentieth century, several important reforms made the Chinese language easier to learn, and made learning more available to a larger number of children. One of the most important of these was the *bai-hua* (pronounced buy-hwa) movement of the 1920s. *Bai-hua* emphasized writing books and newspapers in modern spoken Chinese rather than in the classical form, which was often highly compressed and difficult to interpret. This movement also influenced educators, who prepared teaching materials that reduced the number of years of schooling necessary to understand written materials.

After the 1949 revolution, the educational authorities embarked on an even more ambitious program: They decided to simplify how Chinese characters were written. They took about 2,000 characters and greatly simplified their written forms by reducing the number of strokes needed to write them. Chinese students could now learn their language in a much shorter time and could read simplified-character books and newspapers with much greater ease. Another innovation was the use of *pin yin,* or romanized versions of Chinese characters that could be pronounced by those who could not read the character yet. The *pin yin* system also helped minority children and adults whose native language was not Chinese gain literacy in that language more rapidly; it also helped those who spoke regional dialects of Chinese to learn the national pronunciation of Mandarin (or *putonghua,* pronounced poo-tohng-hwa; see Chapter 1).

One of China's great successes during the 1950s and 1960s was the spread of literacy to almost all urban children and rural children in many regions. The emphasis on **social equality** during various social and economic movements (Land Reform, the Great Leap Forward, the Cultural Revolution) had major effects on education. Education in the countryside had traditionally only been reserved for the landlord and merchant classes, usually because they were the only ones who could afford to pay their children's tuition. The Communist Party attempted to spread educational opportunity to the children of peasants and workers as a means of solidifying support for their social and political programs as well as serving as a means of human resource development for future economic progress.

China has faced a number of problems in deciding what the postelementary curriculum should be. Traditional Chinese schools emphasized a very broad, abstract, liberal arts approach to high school and college education. Education was to train gentlemen and officials in the Confucian classics, with a few useful modern topics (mathematics, science, geography, and so on) thrown in. The Soviet model, which the Chinese Communist Party admired, placed a major emphasis on highly specific technical and scientific training and political education. China has stressed both kinds of approaches since 1949, with varying degrees of success (Savada and Dolan 1988).

China also faced problems in how education should be distributed, especially in rural areas. In the 1950s, it was not possible to establish schools everywhere, so they tended to be established in larger villages and small towns, many of which had school buildings even before 1949. As a result, children from smaller and poorer villages often missed out on educational opportunities, and this increased social inequality in the countryside (Parish and Whyte 1978: 78).

During the 1960s, education at the middle-school level and above became an ideological battleground. Mao Zedong and his supporters mobilized millions of students in his struggle against the party bureaucracy in 1966. These students were told to form Red Guard detachments and to seek out "revisionists," "counterrevolutionaries," and others who might threaten the Maoist revolution. They started by attacking school authorities and teachers and eventually attacked party bureaucrats as well (Heng and Shapiro 1983).

For almost a decade (1966–76), Chinese secondary schools and higher education were in constant turmoil, and Chinese young people (those now in their mid-40s to mid-50s) received very deficient educations. During the Cultural Revolution "people-run schools" brought education to many poor villages, and lower-middle school education spread much more widely in the countryside, even if the quality was often deficient due to a lack of resources and qualified teachers.

During the mid-1970s, secondary schools were gradually reorganized; and after 1976, national examinations for university entrance were reestablished. During the 1980s, the government was well aware of how far it had to go to catch up; it even tolerated letting large numbers of Chinese students attend graduate school in the universities of its erstwhile ideological opponent, the United States.

HOW THE CHINESE EDUCATIONAL SYSTEM WORKS

Although some Chinese children, primarily in urban areas, begin preschool education at age three and one-half, most start their primary education at age seven. Typically, they attend school for six days per week and have a long vacation during July and August. Students in poorer rural areas often only attend school for half a day, then return home to work on the family farm or elsewhere.

The chance to attend and complete high school or college usually depends on how rich a student's home area is as well as on how well he or she achieves in school. Students must pass major examinations to pass from high school to college; just as in many areas of the world, the score on the examination is usually far more important for entrance than grades in school classes.

School Life

Most Chinese junior and senior high school students must wear uniforms to school, and their school life is fairly regimented. Courses in Marxism-Leninism and the history of the Chinese Communist Party are required. In class, teachers lecture most of the time; students do not ask many questions, and there is little class discussion, except in a few courses like political study. Emphasis is still placed on rote learning, and teachers and fellow students are quick to criticize views that are perceived as deviant.

Yet with the opening to the rest of the world since the early 1980s, schools have been unable to control students as well as they could in the first 30 years after 1949. Students are much more exposed to the mass media, especially the Western and Hong Kong media, in recent years. A youth culture has emerged, with its own pop stars. Cui Jian, "China's Bob Dylan" (Kristof and WuDunn 1994: 286) is generally considered to be the first home-grown rock star to emerge in China during the 1980s, singing songs of love and a mild degree of individualistic alienation. Singers like him, including the Chinese-language rock and pop singers from Hong Kong and Taiwan, are well-known among educated Chinese urban youth. They are increasingly tolerated by the political authorities even if older Communist Party members see their message as too individualistic, bourgeois, and occasionally subversive.

The Declining Link between School and Work

The United States differs from many other nations in the degree to which schooling leads naturally into work. In nations like Germany, students in technical high schools begin apprenticeships with major employers even before they graduate. In China, urban junior middle schools and high schools often developed links between various school technical programs and future employers. A factory might take a certain proportion of the graduating class each year. Although employment in urban China was "guaranteed" for many school-leavers through the mid-1980s, in reality many spent a considerable time after graduation looking for suitable employment. In rural areas, school-leavers had a choice of looking for work in local industries or returning to their home production team for employment in farming.

The economic reforms of the 1980s changed the school and work linkage, especially in urban areas. The link between school and factory became less important; a more Western-style **labor market** emerged (see Chapter 5). School-leavers now had to apply for work at different firms and factories just like everyone else, and schools could no longer guarantee employment to their graduates (Bian and Ang 1966).

As the private service and industrial sectors boomed, the link between school and work became more tenuous. Just as in the United States, sometimes those thought of by teachers and administrators as the most unlikely to succeed were the ones who struck it rich. Success in the new China of the 1980s and 1990s was often built on entrepreneurial skills that public schools and colleges have never been very good at teaching: timing, not listening to your elders, hard bargaining, petty bribery, and knowing when to cut your losses. A system designed to turn out politically orthodox bureaucrats for state enterprises is not necessarily what China needs for future growth (see Chapter 10). It may be a tribute to the irrepressible individualism of Chinese youth that so many of them turned out to be such good **entrepreneurs** after years of incarceration in a school system designed to discourage risk taking.

School and Society

China made impressive progress in increasing primary school attendance since 1949. Before then, only about 20 percent of children attended school. Yet by the early 1980s, while the government estimated that nine out of ten children began primary school, only about six graduated, and of those six, only about three met minimum standards of literacy and educational competence.

In China, school attendance does not always correlate with literacy. Social surveys in the mid-1980s among the rural population showed that only when respondents had completed fourth grade did more than 50 percent of them report that they were currently able to read a newspaper or magazine. Even with the simplification of written Chinese characters undertaken after 1949, literacy in Chinese still probably takes a longer time to achieve and (perhaps requires more access to and study of other written materials) than does literacy in alphabetically based languages.

Illiteracy and semiliteracy (Chinese censuses merge these two categories) among adults also continue to be nagging problems in China. In 1990, 15.7 percent of all men and 37.1 percent of all women were illiterate and semiliterate. Given the low level of schooling in pre-1949 China, it is not surprising to find that most of the elderly are illiterate, but even at age 45–49 more than half of all women and almost a fifth of all men are illiterate or semiliterate. At age 20–24 years in 1990, well past the era when the Cultural Revolution was disrupting education, 3.8 percent of all men and 11.9 percent of women were still only semiliterate or illiterate (Population Census Office 1993b: 278–93).

Paradoxically, as China has gotten richer over the past two decades, relatively little has been done to improve primary school education. In fact, the return to family farming that accompanied the agricultural responsibility system stripped power and resources away from local governments, which were responsible for supporting local schools. In many poor rural areas, teachers are paid late or are given salary checks that are very difficult to cash because local governments lack the money to honor them (Ma Rong 1996, personal communication). In addition, the declining financial power of local governments has resulted in less money for schools and more fees imposed on parents of school children. As a result, primary school attendance may have declined, particularly among girls. The new system of family farming may also lead parents to keep children at home as workers. Although official statistics report near-universal elementary school attendance, reports by Chinese and Western observers suggest that many rural children drop out, or are pulled out, of school after only a few years (Kristof and WuDunn 1994: 222–24).

The Chinese government has attempted to encourage the spread of universal middle school attendance (through grade nine) in the major cities and in the richer coastal provinces. These areas have been able to provide more opportunities for junior high and senior high school students to complete their education, but in poorer provinces or counties these chances are often lacking. The gap between the best and the worst provinces, municipalities, and autonomous areas in China can be seen in Table 4–1. In the best-educated regions (the municipalities of Beijing, Tianjin, and Shanghai, and Liaoning and Jilin provinces

TABLE 4-1

Distribution of Education in Five Best-Educated and Five Worst-Educated Provinces of China (1990 census data)

	Graduates per 100 Population		
	University	Senior Middle School	Junior Middle School
Best-educated			
Beijing municipality	5.5	14.3	30.2
Shanghai municipality	3.2	15.3	30.9
Tianjin municipality	2.1	11.9	29.0
Liaoning province	1.0	8.7	32.2
Jilin province	0.9	10.2	26.1
Worst-educated			
Tibet autonomous region	0.2	0.7	2.9
Henan province	0.3	6.0	26.4
Hainan province	0.3	8.2	21.0
Guangxi-Zhuang			
autonomous region	0.3	5.5	19.0
Shandong province	0.3	5.7	25.1

Source: Population Census Office, 1993a: 36–37.

in the northeast), about one out of every three or four people is a junior middle school graduate. Yet in most of the poorly educated provinces, about one out of four or five people is also a graduate; only Tibet lags behind here. Of course, these data say nothing about the quality of schooling, which can vary widely.

The largest gap between the provinces and municipalities is at the senior middle school (equivalent to high school in the United States) and university-graduate level. Out of every 100 people in the three big cities and well-educated provinces like Jilin and Liaoning, from 1 to 5 people were university graduates and 9 to 15 people were senior middle school graduates. In the worst-educated provinces, only about 1 out of every 300 to 500 people were university graduates, and only about 1 to 8 people per 100 were senior middle school graduates.

IMPROVING THE EDUCATIONAL SYSTEM

Although China has been more successful than nations like India or Pakistan in spreading primary school education to rural areas, much of the talk of China as an emerging economic superpower ignores one central fact. Becoming an economic superpower requires a very well educated population, and here China doesn't measure up. In 1990, 6.138 million of the 789.235 million Chinese age 6 or older were university graduates, or

0.78 percent (Population Census Office 1993b: 112–15). In other words, fewer than one out of every hundred Chinese was a college graduate.

Since China is an underdeveloped nation, we might think that there has been a significant improvement in levels of college attendance over time, and recent age **cohorts** have done better. Among those age 60 in 1990 (those who were born in 1930 and completed college about 1952), 1.49 percent were college graduates. Among those age 24 (born in 1966 and completed college about 1988), there were 1.28 percent college graduates. Between 1952 and 1988, rates of college graduation may have actually declined.

The figures look even worse when we factor in the effects of the Cultural Revolution. The age group that is 43 to 51 years old in 1998 (a key group in terms of providing China's managers, scientists, and administrators for the next decade or so) was heavily affected by the virtual shutdown of most of China's universities from 1966–76. This group, born between 1947 and 1955, had a rate of college attendance of only 0.47 percent; in other words, less than one out of every two hundred completed university training.

By way of comparison, in the United States in 1990 about 30 percent of 60-year-olds, 37 percent of 40–44-year-olds, and about 30 percent of 24-year-olds were college graduates (see Anderton et al. 1997: 498). Among Americans, the proportion of college graduates usually rises from the early 20s to the mid-30s (by as much as 10–15 percent), as people return to complete college as adults. In China, these kinds of opportunities are very limited; for the vast majority of people, the education that they have by about age 22 is the highest level that they will ever attain. Only recently have alternative sources of college education for adults (television universities, workers' universities, and so on) become available to Chinese who did not pass the highly competitive college entrance examinations, and these schools can only serve a small number of students.

Even by comparison with other developing nations, China's achievement in higher education is not very impressive. One common cross-national measure of the effort a society devotes to higher education is the number of college students as a proportion of all youth ages 18–21 years. In China in 1990, there were 2.8 million college students (counting both university and junior-college students), or 2.87 percent of all young people age 18–21 (Population Census Office 1993a: 33–34). In India, the equivalent figure is 8 percent, and even in such extremely poor nations as Vietnam and Burma about 2 percent of youth attend college. One remarkable aspect of the post-1978 economic revolution is that this may be the first case in which a nation undergoing rapid economic development was virtually stagnant in the area of higher education. Chinese universities are surprisingly small (world-famous Peking University only has about 10,000 undergraduates), and few have expanded since the early 1980s.

Universities as Growth Engines

In the United States, many planners now recognize that a university can be a growth pole of economic development. Quite often, creative, entrepreneurial people are attracted to university communities, which tend to be more tolerant of quirky and inventive people; or universities spin off such folks themselves, like the nth year graduate student who develops a best-selling software product.

Whether universities will serve the same function in China is hard to say. They are usually gated communities: University security guards can check entrants for an identification badge. One can't "hang out" at the university library very easily; undergraduate students are not allowed access to the library stacks; and book budgets are so tight that universities must often rely on foreign donations, often from Overseas Chinese alumni and friends, for up-to-date journals and books.

In a few cases, like the Haidian district of Beijing that surrounds Peking University (nicknamed Bei-da), the presence of a university has resulted in significant economic development. In this area, which also includes the campuses of Qinghua University (China's M.I.T.) and eight other major universities, there are computer factories, software development firms, and retail computer shops. A number were started by former faculty members or students from Bei-da, and some retain ties to various university departments. However, while this district may give us a glimpse into a future Chinese Silicon Valley, it is not very representative of the usual relations between private firms, state enterprises, and state-run higher education in most parts of China.

Sending Students Abroad: Catch-Up or Brain Drain?

China tried to develop a group of trained technical experts during the 1980s and early 1990s by sending its advanced students to the United States and other nations. In this way, it could obtain students trained in the latest techniques of their branch of science without a huge investment in research and development costs within China.

Yet there were several problems with this strategy. A large number of these students discovered ways to stay in the United States and other nations after completing their degrees. They found it difficult to return to China; many had no wish to return to a repressive political system, and many discovered that they could make more money than they ever dreamed possible in jobs outside China. About 40,000 Chinese students, and their dependents, were given permission to remain in the United States after the suppression of the democratic student movement in China in 1989, and few of them have returned to China permanently.

Returning graduate students encountered other problems as well. Even for those who want to return and use their skills in China, university or government laboratories are often so poorly equipped and under-funded that they can do little research. In addition, some returning students find that their colleagues and superiors who have not gone abroad resent their expertise and put obstacles in the way of their research.

Part of the problem is a sociological one: To successfully complete their graduate degrees abroad, many Chinese students began to think in terms of **professions.** In this mind-set, one's primary orientation is toward one's profession, not toward any particular employer. The opinions of colleagues, even those in different institutions or other countries, often are valued as highly as those of one's immediate superiors. Many find the more freewheeling, individualistic approach to research, and to life in general, that they discovered in Western universities to be attractive. This professional, individualistic orientation does not mesh well with the hierarchical, bureaucratic, and group-oriented organizational style of most Chinese universities and research bureaucracies.

SUMMARY

China did a remarkable job of spreading basic education to the countryside in the 1950s, but much of the effort stalled during the 1960s. Illiteracy and semiliteracy remain serious problems for the adult population today, and there appears to be a widening gulf between rich and poor areas in basic education, especially for girls. At the secondary level, China also has been able to broaden access to education, but universal junior middle school attendance only seems to be an attainable goal for cities and some of the rural areas of richer provinces. With the growth of a largely nonpolitical, consumer-oriented youth culture, especially in urban areas, schools now exert less power over the lives of their students.

While China's universities produce many outstanding students, there are few of them in proportion to the size of the population. A good number go abroad for further training and never return to China to work. China still faces problems in adapting its educational system to the nation's current economic realities. The dynamism is in the private sector, but little in the curriculum or the method of teaching encourages new ways of thinking, risk taking, or an entrepreneurial spirit. In many areas of science, research in Chinese universities still lags behind world standards.

CHAPTER 5

The Family and Marriage

There has been a slow transition in the lives of most Chinese from a traditional society in which an individual's life choices were primarily governed by his or her family to one in which they were governed by the family and the state, and now to one in which they are governed by the family, state, and the individual's own desires and capabilities. Although there have been striking changes in marriage and the family over the past half-century, the family remains the major economic and social institution in China. Similarly, while control over marriage has shifted away from elders in the family toward the individual and the state, almost all Chinese women and a vast majority of men still marry. As will be seen below, the path toward the modernization of marriage and family patterns in China has been a very different route from that taken in Western capitalist nations.

Family and marriage in traditional China were major institutions by which the patriarchal system controlled the lives of men, women, and children. However, the forms of marriage and family differed greatly between the gentry (rich land- or capital-owning families) and the rest of society (chiefly peasants and artisans). Family organization and kinds of marriages could also differ between regions of traditional China and between historical eras. What will be described below is an **ideal type** of the major forms of marriage and family among the majority Han people (see Chapter 1) before the twentieth century. The twentieth century brought remarkable changes in family organization, both before and after the Communist Party's victory in 1949.

FAMILIES IN CHINESE HISTORY

The family is a key unit in the Confucian tradition. Chinese law recognized that family obligations, particularly of a son to his father or elder brother, took precedence in many cases over civil or legal ones. Yet even within these traditions of hierarchy, there was some recognition of rights as well as obligations. While younger brothers were obliged to respect their older brothers, all brothers were supposed to share equally in inheritance. While all sons were supposed to venerate their fathers, in cases of irreconcilable disagreements sons could ask for a breakup of the family estate (*fen-jia*, pronounced fehn-jah) so that each could get a share.

In many societies, norms can differ from actual practice, and in studying Chinese society it is often dangerous to make assumptions about how social life was conducted from upper-class norms. Recent research into Japanese colonial household registers from Taiwan (a surprisingly accurate source of data on Chinese family formation and dissolution from 1905–43) has shown that illegitimacy, divorce, marriage of husbands into their wives' families, and remarriage of women after widowhood were fairly common even if forbidden or disparaged by Confucian norms.

Both Chinese religion and a life spent close to the edge of existence made Chinese families very aware of the necessity of designing a strategy for family survival. Chinese ancestor worship says that in order for the deceased ancestors to avoid becoming hungry ghosts, members of the current generation with the same surname must make daily and annual sacrifices for them. Ancestor worship does not command Chinese to have *many* sons; in fact, that can dissipate family wealth. Rather, there should be at least *one surviving son* in each generation to carry on the family name and to conduct these sacrifices.

Another important social fact about Chinese families is that law is thicker than blood. The Chinese have long recognized that in a society where having a male descendant is extremely important, this event cannot be left to the vagaries of biology. Adoption of the children of close kin, friends, and strangers has a long history in China and is perfectly legal. Strangely enough, China's neighbors, the equally Confucian Koreans, have never had a tradition of nonkin adoption; for them, blood kinship is usually the only acceptable form.

Different Aspects of Chinese Families

The Chinese family is a set of at least four interlocking social networks, none of which overlap exactly in space and time:

- *The ritual family:* These are the actual relatives of an individual. When an important event like a funeral occurs, family members of different degrees of kinship attend. In a traditional Chinese funeral procession, the degrees of kinship (to the deceased) are marked by the roughness of the weave of the burlap clothing worn by the kin (the closest relatives wear the roughest weave). The ritual family also includes all the dead ancestors and yet-to-be-born descendants. The former deserve sacrifices to protect their place in heaven and to prevent them from becoming hungry ghosts; the latter deserve to have the family fortune protected so that it may be handed down to them.

- *The residential family:* This is the group of family members who share the same dwelling. Things can get complicated here, because, increasingly, sharing the same dwelling does not always mean being part of what Americans might refer to as the family circle, those with whom daily joys and sorrows are shared openly. Increasingly, in both city and country, the older generation may share the same dwelling unit, but often neither they nor their coresident adult children consider themselves to be sharing this closer definition of family (the *jia-ting cheng-yuan,* pronounced jah-tihng-chung-u-ahn).

- *The economic family:* There are members of the family who are not coresident (such as a younger brother in another city) but who may have a claim on family financial resources. After the death of a parent, for example, both coresident and non-coresident brothers share in the estate. In a society without a banking system willing to make unsecured loans to individuals, these kinds of claims can be very important as a financial resource.

- *The family of affect:* Even though Confucian ideology emphasizes that only paternal relatives are important, children spend a good part of their early years with their mothers. These mothers keep in contact with their family of orientation, those relatives with whom they grew up before marriage. Today it is not uncommon for Chinese to have strong bonds with their mothers' kin. In some sense it is easier, because the bond is usually made on the basis of affection rather than obligation, and it is a more playful kind of kinship. Mother's younger brother (*su-su,* pronounced sue-sue) can play and have fun with his niece or nephew, whereas father's brothers always feel that they also have a responsibility to train them in family traditions.

Margery Wolf (1972) proposed that much of a woman's real power in traditional Chinese families lies in her ability to create a "uterine family," or a family of biological, or sometimes adopted, descendants within the larger patriarchal family. These biological or adopted descendants have strong emotional ties (affect) with their mother and support her position in the family. If a father wanted to take a concubine and his wife opposed it, then his son might also support his mother by opposing it. Wolf's explanation of Chinese family dynamics is a useful tool in understanding the role of fertility for different family members. Chinese wives wanted children, especially sons, not just because their relatives told them that this was their major job in life but also because having children created allies in the next generation who could protect their position in the family.

The family of affect can also cut across other kinds of ties. In many upper-class families, where several adult brothers lived together with their wives and children, cousins (especially those close in age) could grow up as close as brothers in Western families. A successful uncle might finance his poorer nephew's education; this could create a strong emotional bond as well. Close women friends sometimes pledge their children to one another in a kind of fictive kinship arrangement (this is called *gan ma*, pronounced gahn-mah, or "dry mother"). The fictive kin pledges that she will help raise the child if anything happens to the mother, and she becomes a sort of godmother to the child even while the real mother is alive.

Types of Families

Sociologists and family historians usually divide families into three kinds of residential units: **nuclear families,** composed of one set of parents and their minor children; **stem families,** made up of one set of grandparents, one set of parents (including one of the grandparents' children), and the parents' minor children; and **grand, or extended, families,** where one set of grandparents, a number of sets of parents (including two or more of their children and their spouses), and the children of these parents live together. In China, as in every other past and present society, some proportion of the population lived in each of these three kinds of residential units. In addition, some Chinese lived as single-person households, or as family fragments (such as a mother and her son or an uncle and his nephew residing together), or even as groups of unrelated individuals. What distinguished traditional China from other societies was the great emphasis in the societal value system on the importance of family coresidence.

For Chinese, the ideal was "five generations under one roof," or a highly extended family that lived together in harmony. The ideal here was to have all of the married brothers, and their wives and children, living together in one coresident unit. Yet the high and unstable death rates found in any traditional society meant that few family members reached the age at which they could become grandparents, much less great-grandparents; the ideal five-generation family would, after all, require some members to reach the age of great-great-grandparents. For most peasant families, lack of resources forced some children to find economic opportunities elsewhere. Finally, while Chinese norms stressed family harmony and obedience to the wishes of the eldest male members, such harmony was often difficult to achieve. The Chinese had clear customs regarding how a family and its property could be divided if conflicts between its members grew too great.

No person was a member of a nuclear, stem, or grand family (or of a family fragment) forever. During people's lives their families might pass through many different forms as economic and social circumstances caused families to grow, contract, or split.

Clans and Lineages

For many Chinese males, much of their identity revolved around membership in a particular family, often a family with deep historical roots. In traditional China, many males were part of a *lineage*, a group of people who could show, usually through written records or oral history, that they were descended from particular ancestors. A group of such related lineages was referred to as a *clan*. Clans shared the same surname and often shared property, such as a clan temple or clan-owned farmland, which could be rented to clan members or outsiders. As a result, clan elders or leaders had a great deal of power over other clan members. In a society in which clans and lineages held such power, it was difficult to develop trust in outsiders (who usually belonged to competing clans), or conversely, to be trusted by outsiders.

In some regions of China, especially in the southeastern provinces of Fujian and Guangdong, this emphasis on lineage led to the development of villages where virtually all inhabitants were members of the same clan. In such *single-surname villages,* the economic, social, and religious functions of the community overlapped with the functions of the family, both ensnaring and protecting the individual within the web of kinship. For many other Chinese, particularly peasants in multisurnamed villages in north China, clan or lineage ties had less importance as a possible means of obtaining resources or as focal point for identification. For them, village and nuclear or stem family membership usually determined access to resources.

Between the north China ideal type of little lineage or clan extension and the southeastern clan villages, there were a variety of other types of arrangements. For example, in Luts'un (or in *pin yin* romanization, *lucun,* pronounced loo-swun), the village in Yunnan province studied by Xiaotong Fei and Chih-I Chang in the mid-1940s, about 75 percent of the farmland was owned by individual landowners. Of the rest, about 40 percent was owned (and leased out) by six clans or lineages, and the rest was owned by various religious groups (Temple to the Lord of Earth, Hong Chiao Kong Temple) and fraternal or educational societies (Taoist Music Society, Confucius Club, Fraternity of Honesty and Righteousness, and so on; see Fei and Chang 1948: 55). In this case, no one clan dominated the village, but affiliation with the Wang or Wei clans (the two major landowners) would probably give one's family some economic benefits.

The Family and the State

The family was both the key supporting institution and a major problem for the Chinese state. In most villages there were no government officials; instead, the state relied on clan elders to help keep order. In multisurnamed villages, this often meant that disputes between villagers of different surnames had to be settled by the elders of the families on the two sides. This would often involve some kind of ceremony, such as a dinner, at which some admission of responsibility by one or both sides would be made and pledges of good feeling and good behavior toward the other side would be exchanged, and sometimes even honored. Conflicts between single-surnamed villages could be much more serious affairs, sometimes escalating into affrays in which dozens of clan members might be killed or wounded over decades. These conflicts were often over economic advantage (fights over irrigation rights were a common cause), but they could result from more trivial causes as well.

The state held families responsible for the crimes of their members. This mutual responsibility system, called the *bao-jia* (pronounced bow-jah) system, required that clan elders or other clan members serve the prison term, or be executed, in the place of any clan member who escaped before punishment. This system was used under a number of dynasties. Yet while the Chinese family might seem to be an ideal vehicle for social control, it could also serve as a way of subverting the government. The Chinese state recognized, and taught, that everyone should follow the five key relationships in society: father-son, elder brother–younger brother, ruler-ruled, husband-wife, and friend to friend. However, the need to help other family members advance and prosper, regardless of merit, meant that government service could become a major source of corrupt funds for the family. *Mandarins* (those who passed the imperial examination and were appointed as officials) were never appointed to administer any part of their home provinces, and they were usually rotated from place to place every three years to reduce the power their families might exert over them.

In many areas, rich families became virtually law unto themselves. Conflicts due to landlord exploitation of tenants could boil up into full-scale peasant revolts against the government. The strong norms about helping family members could also lead families of rebels or criminals to hide them rather than turn them over to the local courts.

The family also had powerful symbolism for those on the margins of society as well. Those without a family (due to expulsion from a family, orphanhood, fleeing from criminal prosecution, and so on) were at the mercy of almost anyone. Criminal gangs and secret societies were often organized on a pseudo-kinship basis: Important and powerful members were often referred to as *elder brother,* with the authority to command obedience. A famous Chinese novel, *Shui Hu Zhuan* (pronounced shwei-hoo-juahn; *Water Margin Novel,* also translated by Pearl Buck as *All Men Are Brothers),* was about such a group of hero-bandits; reportedly it was Mao Zedong's favorite piece of classical literature.

THE COMMUNIST REVOLUTION AND THE FAMILY

The new policies instituted by the Communist Party in China's villages had their most profound effect on clans and lineages: They virtually eliminated them (Yang 1965). Clan and lineage ceremonies were forbidden, often-secret books that showed clan relationships and genealogies were exposed and then burned, and their temples were destroyed. During the Land Reform Campaign, clan elders were attacked as part of the landlord classes; they were publicly vilified and often physically attacked and executed. This campaign (in which 700,000 or more landlords may have been killed) in the early 1950s was so thorough that, whatever else happens in rural China over the next few decades, it is next to impossible that the descendants of these clan and lineage leaders will ever hold significant amounts of power.

One problem that the Communist Party faced in the early 1950s was that, after receiving land during the Land Reform Campaign, all that many poor farmers wanted to do was buy a wife and start on the road to getting rich themselves. It soon became apparent that bringing the revolution to the ordinary family life of most peasants was going to be a far more difficult task. Many of the struggles the party experienced in agricultural policy (see Chapter 3) were as much about the stubborn focus of Chinese farmers on the immediate survival and welfare of their own families as they were about how various units were to be organized (Yang 1996). In many cases, the party had to tolerate traditional ways of organizing families or local customs (Parish and Whyte 1978).

Of course, the family provided certain benefits to the state as well. The family provided a ready-made institution for the care of the dependent population. In fact, the obligation for children, especially sons, to support their elderly parents and disabled family members is codified in Chinese law, and the state could rely on families to pay for their children's educational and medical expenses (DeGlopper 1988: 130). The pooling of income found in Chinese families gave the state a solution to the problem of how to match production and consumption in a way that would be acceptable to the population. Since the establishment of the Responsibility System in agriculture in 1978 (Chapter 9), the family has reasserted many of its pre-1949 functions in terms of production, consumption, and distribution, and the role of state agencies has declined.

CHINESE FAMILY SIZE

In societies with high death rates, even when families try to stay together they can never get very large because they run out of surviving members. John Lossing Buck's monumental (1937) study of Chinese farm families found that the mean size of coresident families was about 5.2 people. By the time of the 1953 census, average Chinese family size had dropped to 4.30 (Zeng 1992: 536). However, this 1953 figure included urban families, which are usually smaller, and was also affected by the 1950–53 land reform, which tended to split up both poor and rich families.

As several anthropologists have pointed out, during the 1950s and 1960s China experienced "family convergence" (DeGlopper 1988: 130–31, Davis and Harrell 1993: 7). The distribution of land to poor and hitherto landless farmers allowed them to marry, to let more of their children survive, and to have more of their parents to survive into old age and to live with them. Average family size grew between 1950 and 1978 for demographic reasons, because more people were surviving; but it grew for social structural ones as well, because almost no one was allowed to migrate away from communes or production brigades. The increasing urbanization of the Chinese population should have led to shrinking family sizes, but housing shortages made it difficult for newly married couples to form new residential units. By the mid-1980s, in major urban areas like Beijing and Guangzhou, about 20 percent of recently married couples had to live with the bride's parents, a situation known as *matrilocal residence* (Barrett, Xu, and Zusman 1993: 121).

During the 1980s, as migration began to be tolerated and as the One Child Policy began to have an effect, family size began to shrink, especially in rural areas. "In 1980 rural households averaged 5.5 members and urban households 4.4; by 1988 they had fallen to 4.9 and 3.6, respectively" (Davis and Harrell 1993: 7). Yet the shrinkage did not mean that nuclear families were starting to predominate over all other forms. Instead, a number of researchers have found that the rapidly changing economic environment in China (see Chapters 8–10) had major effects on family formation and structure as well. The family has once again become a unit of production, adding or shedding coresident members as economic circumstances warrant.

In the future, family formation may be more affected by current economic advantage than either by demographic constraints or government policies. With China's increase in life expectancy (Chapter 2), the vast majority of young people in the future will have surviving parents, grandparents, and possibly great-grandparents. Whereas in the recent past the government would have forced kin to live together, in the future many of the elderly will have enough money to live on their own.

With the economic possibility of separate residence of the elderly, what will Chinese families do? Taiwan, which has already reached this demographic and economic crossroads, has shown us one pattern: A very large proportion of the elderly still live with their younger kin (Thornton and Lin 1994). Yet Taiwan's land reform and economic development program, as well as its family value structure, is quite different from that of China. In many areas of China, especially urban ones, it appears that it is more the housing shortage than the pull of obligation that keeps the generations living together, and this could change rapidly.

THE ONE-CHILD FAMILY

Chinese economic development, especially rural development since 1978, has been of major historical importance, but the improvement in the living standards of individuals in China has been closely linked to the success of the birth planning program. For example, if a nation's economy is growing at 4 percent a year, and its population is growing at 3 percent a year, then the real growth in per-person income is only 1 percent a year. China's huge increases in growth (on the order of 8–11 percent per year over the last decade) are even more impressive because annual population growth rates have been below 1.5 percent per year since the late 1970s (see Chapters 1 and 2). Real income growth, then, has been averaging about 6–8 percent per year, a far higher rate of real economic growth per person than is true of most Third World nations.

Most educated Chinese are aware that there is a strong linkage between the population planning program and continued economic progress. The paradox is that the population planning program, with its centralized control at the national or provincial level, is a relic of the pre-reform political structure. Its intrusiveness into the everyday life of individuals and its reliance on propaganda, threat, and coercion rather than market forces to get couples to comply with national goals for births may become less and less effective. The birth control regulations of 1979 that established the One-Child Policy had major implications for Chinese families. "In one stroke of the bureaucratic pen, Chinese leaders decided that henceforth only half of all families would have a son to carry on the family name, that the sibling relationship would disappear, and that failure to use contraception would be a punishable offense" (Davis and Harrell 1993: 3). From that point on, there was direct state intervention in one of the family's most basic tasks, reproduction.

Can China continue to keep the birth rate low? Currently the answer appears to be: in the cities, yes; in the rural areas, maybe. In urban areas, the one-child family has become the norm for almost all resident couples. There is strong normative pressure to have only one child. Housing shortages in urban areas make it difficult to raise more than one child, and possible penalties (especially educational penalties against second- or higher-order children) affect behavior as well. Most urban women are now educated at least through the junior high school level, and a large proportion of women are employed (Chapter 7). In urban China, as in the United States, the combination of educational and job opportunities for women appears to be a very powerful force in encouraging a low birth rate, and this decline might have taken place without the strong government-sponsored one-child family planning program.

Parents in Chinese cities are not so concerned about having a son with whom to live in old age. Most urban residents can keep their housing after retirement, many receive some sort of pension, and many find that, just as in Western nations, adult daughters who live nearby also keep in close contact with them and provide needed services (Bian, Logan, and Bian 1998). In cities, the pressure for housing forces a large proportion of young married couples to live with their parents in cramped apartments, and the birth of a child only adds to the space squeeze. Thus government pressure, increased expectations for consumer

The Zhang family at a gathering in 1998. Note the few children, the large proportion of surviving elderly and middle-aged members, and the variety of styles in clothing and coiffure.

goods, a shortage of housing, educational aspirations for children, and a growing acceptance of gender equality all help to increase compliance with the one-child family goal.

In rural areas the situation is very different. China lacks a social security system for its rural workers; in fact, the post-1978 responsibility system has made the system of Chinese farming much more individualistic. This household individualism has resulted in a huge surge in productivity and profits for rural households, but it has also made them aware that they are dependent on their own resources for retirement income—which usually means they must rely on a coresident son. Although China has a vast rural labor surplus (see Chapter 9), the average farm family is acutely aware that prosperity in old age is dependent on producing a son.

In rural China today, there is a rough compromise between the government and the population on acceptable levels of fertility. Since the government has not instituted any significant old-age support program, it tolerates couples who have a second child if the first child is "unsatisfactory," that is, if the first one is female, a male with a birth defect, or a child who dies. Couples who try to have a second child after a satisfactory male child can get into serious trouble. Those who have two female children often find that they have a serious problem: They want a male child, but having three children clearly violates government rules as well.

Female Infanticide and
Sex-Selective Abortion

China is the only nation in the world with such punitive birth control laws. And although those laws have lowered the Chinese birth rate, they have also led to forced abortions, sex-selective abortions, and **female infanticide.** The sex ratios of young children reported in Chinese censuses and surveys of the 1980s and 1990s in several Chinese provinces indicate that there are many missing girls, especially among second- or later-parity children. For the early 1980s, there is little doubt that female infanticide was widespread in the rural areas of many provinces. Since that time, the picture is less clear. Sex-selective abortion, usually after an ultrasound determines the sex of the fetus, has become much more common. In addition, farm families are now better able to hide the birth of a female child, and local officials are less likely to report births that fall "outside the plan" to higher authorities. While ideologues on either side of the female infanticide question talk about it with great certainty, we know of no demographer who has even attempted to measure the amount of female infanticide in China over the past decade because the data are so unreliable.

The Future of Birth Planning

What will the growth of the Chinese economy and the increasing prosperity of Chinese do to the success of the birth planning program? At present, couples who have too many children must pay fines or suffer penalties, such as having to pay tuition for children attending state-run schools or denial of entry into schools for later children. Increasing rural prosperity means that these fines and penalties for having too many children may become increasingly ineffective as a way to motivate the rural population. Normative means of control, such as propaganda, may also become less effective as the communications media become more oriented toward commercial messages and entertainment. In many areas, family planning workers are already the most unpopular people in the countryside, so coercion may only increase opposition to the government.

The government has tried to enforce family planning goals by making the attainment of these goals one of the major yardsticks by which the competence of a rural official is judged. Lower-level administrators who tolerate a large number of births beyond the first or second child are setting themselves up for no promotion, or sometimes demotion, from their posts. As a result, these officials often pressure farm families to have fewer children at the same time as their organizational tools to force such compliance are of declining value. One result is that some officials are reporting fewer births than actually occurred. In recent months, there are indications that some officials are ignoring individual violations of birth planning regulations as long as the overall level of fertility remains at moderate levels (*Chicago Tribune* May 24, 1998).

The experience of several other East Asian nations suggests that two structural variables are important in making rural dwellers want to have fewer children rather than just forcing them to do so. Educating women allows them to have more say in family decision making and helps them better understand contraception and its effective use. Educated daughters can also make significant contributions to the family income. Giving rural parents the idea that their children have a real opportunity for social mobility, which usually means giving them a chance at getting an urban or off-farm job, will also lead them to have fewer children. If parents believe that there is a chance for social mobility through education or business, they may wish to provide fewer children a better education or scarce capital with which to start a business, or what demographers call the quality versus quantity trade-off.

MARRIAGE AND MATE SELECTION

According to traditional Chinese norms, especially upper-class ones, marriages were to be arranged by parents and the bride and groom were to meet at the wedding. Although Chinese families were often interested in improving their status or economic position by having a child "marry up," it is clear that if everyone in the marriage market has this goal, not everyone could do so. Instead, most Chinese families were satisfied with "matching doors" with the prospective bride or groom's family, or finding a family of about equivalent social status with whom to form kinship ties. Chinese marriages often were arranged by matchmakers, usually older women who either charged a fee or expected presents for finding a mate with the appropriate social standing. Once the matchmaker had found partners acceptable to both sets of parents, it was often difficult for children to refuse to at least meet with the future partner. Even in traditional China a strong-willed person, especially a man, could refuse a partner, but often another, possibly even less desirable candidate, was waiting in the wings.

The choosing of a marriage partner set in motion an avalanche of customs, advice, and family pressure that both young people often found hard to resist. Fortune-tellers would often aid in determining an auspicious day for the wedding; more than the usual number of weddings were held around the Chinese New Year (in late January or February), but the demands of the agricultural work schedule and other factors could influence the timing of marriages as well (Anderton and Barrett 1990). Staging an expensive wedding, or a funeral for older kin members, was essential to maintaining the family's social status in the community and was one of the few reasons that normally tightfisted peasant families would go into debt.

After the Marriage Law of 1950 went into effect there were significant changes in how marriages took place (Croll 1984). Large wedding feasts, for which families often went deeply into debt, were forbidden as a waste of resources and because they were a feudal custom. Introductions through paid or unofficial matchmakers still took place, often because the young people were too shy to take on this task themselves. In most marriage negotiations after the early 1950s, both the parents and the children could veto the proposed mate: "Few young people are pressured into a match, and few couples marry in defiance of parental wishes" (Parish and Whyte 1978: 173).

The law also forbids child marriage or engagement, which was common in some areas, and youth were to be allowed to pick their own partners. However, no true dating culture emerged. It was hard for young people to be alone together, especially for those who lived in villages full of nosy kinfolk . One sent-down educated youth described the situation in rural Guangdong province in the early 1970s:

> I discovered that in the commune men and women peasants, especially young men and women, very rarely conversed, and all were very shy. Although we intellectual youths all grew up in the city, when we were in this kind of rural setting we also did not dare to violate their traditional customs, and we also rarely conversed with girl members of the team. (Parish and Whyte 1978: 170)

Paradoxically, in some ways it was easier to find a marriage partner than to find a boyfriend or girlfriend. Once one was of the appropriate age, various kinds of go-betweens could be enlisted to find a marriage partner: friends living at a distance, older relatives, former school classmates, and so on. Young men or women would sometimes volunteer to work on projects at distant sites as a way of meeting members of the opposite sex. Yet needless to say, once these kinds of social resources were mobilized, it often became very difficult to back out if one decided one did not really love, or even like, the proposed spouse.

After the Cultural Revolution, the era of Communist asceticism (Chapter 6) when virtually no interest in the opposite sex was allowed, conditions changed in both urban and rural areas. Although Chinese youth have, on average, far fewer boyfriends or girlfriends than do their American counterparts, the networks and introduction mechanisms that lead to marriage are remarkably similar. In both rural and urban areas of China and in the United States, introductions by family members led to a marriage partner for about 15 percent of survey respondents (Liu 1992: 264; Laumann, Gagnon, Michaels, and Michaels 1994: 235). In rural China, introductions by friends or other acquaintances accounted for 53 percent of later marriage partners, compared to 47 percent in urban China and 48 percent in the United States. About a quarter of rural Chinese respondents report finding their marriage partner on their own, compared to 35 percent of urban Chinese and 32 percent of Americans. Thus while some aspects of marriage are different in China (parents still exert more of a veto power), the ways in which Chinese now select mates are not that different from those found in the United States.

In every society, potential partners in the marriage market vary in attractiveness. Before 1949, those of upper class or landlord status were preferred; during the 1949–78 period those working for the government or with well-paid and secure jobs in state enterprises were seen as good catches. During the 1980s and 1990s, the marriage market became more complex (Whyte 1990). Men of previously low status, such as farmers, now often have a good deal of money, whereas those with secure state jobs have little. The unpredictability of the market economy has been transferred to the marriage market; it is hard to tell who is a good bet for future success anymore.

Marriage and Divorce

As was mentioned in Chapter 2, one major continuity of Chinese marriage is that almost all (99 percent or more) of women get married. Due to the One-Child Policy, the peaks and falls in the age at marriage during the 1979–96 period are not of much demographic interest. What is important is that, unlike in Western Europe or the United States, no social role for older unmarried women developed in China. While some women receive advanced education and most expect to work outside the home, almost all Chinese women still expect to marry and have children only within marriage.

Chinese men are usually 2–4 years older than their brides. This fact, combined with the shrinking sizes of birth cohorts since 1980, means that over the next 15 years there will be a severe shortage of women. In the marriage market between now and 2012, there will be a sex ratio of at least 110 males to every 100 females in their mid-20s. Women will have increased bargaining power in this marriage market. The result of this shortage is hard to predict. With no older unmarried women available (since almost all Chinese women marry by age 30), men may have to search for younger women. Eligible women can become more choosy about their future husbands; this will probably leave poor, rural, and ill-educated men at the end of the queue. It could also lead to an increase in divorce rates as women drop men who did not measure up to their expectations.

In fact, divorce rates appear to be rising; certainly, this is the perception of most Chinese. In the past, divorce was difficult to get because it involved a much wider community (relatives, the work unit) than just the two unhappy individuals themselves. Divorce also had wider social and political ramifications (it was usually impossible to get without prolonged mediation sessions conducted by outside authorities), so people shied away from it. With a decline in the state's interference in people's private lives since the early 1980s, divorce has become more common.

Given the economic reforms, increased education of and labor force participation among women, and so on, there is little reason to believe that this trend will decrease, but it does not appear to be a crisis in society. The increased divorce rate may also be due to a greater desire on the part of men and women to find someone with whom they are sexually compatible (Chapter 6), a goal that never received much attention in Chinese society before 1978.

Domestic Abuse

In traditional China, domestic abuse, usually of wives by husbands or by their mothers-in-law, was common, virtually unpunished, and generally sanctioned by the Confucian value system. The marriage and family reforms of the early 1950s reduced the power of families, clans, and lineages, and local branches of the Women's Federation might now intervene on behalf of abused wives; however, domestic abuse appears to have remained common, especially in rural areas of north China. Since this topic has received almost no attention from Chinese or foreign researchers, it is hard to estimate whether domestic abuse has become more or less common after the economic reforms.

The return to family farming and a more family-centered existence may have led to increased spouse abuse, but the rising divorce rate and the increased rates of out-migration across China may point to a greater propensity of women to escape such abuse. The relatively open discussion of Chinese domestic violence at a recent forum on women's issues in Beijing (attended by Hillary Rodham Clinton) in June 1998 was quite different from the lack of attention paid to the topic by Chinese authorities during the International Women's Conference there in 1995 (*Chicago Tribune* June 28, 1998: A-12); this may lead to more government attention to the problem.

SUMMARY

Chinese families and kinship can be defined in a variety of ways. Families differed by social class, region, and historical era. Much of traditional Chinese social organization was based on the patriarchal family. The Communist state destroyed clans and lineages and reorganized families in such a way that there was greater state intervention in family processes, especially in production. The post-1978 Responsibility System has restored many functions to the rural family. Yet in key areas related to recruitment (marriage) and reproduction (the one-child family), the Chinese family has not reverted to traditional patterns. In fact, the new environment will pose new challenges for Chinese families. As journalist Matt Fourney points out, the "one-child policy creates a '1-2-4 phenomenon'—one child, two parents, four grandparents" (*Far Eastern Economic Review* October 23, 1997: 82). There are more older kin members alive now than ever before, but there is also more money available. Rapid economic growth and occupational change have tilted knowledge, and to some degree authority, to the young; they are the natives in the new marketplace.

Marriage is, in some respects, most remarkable for what has not happened. Marriage markets are now more similar to those in other modern nations, but almost everyone still expects to get married. Whether the future shortage of women in the marriage market over the next 15 years will allow men to do so (and how they will adapt if they can't) will be an interesting question. While divorce rates are rising from low levels, this is not seen as a major social problem, and the problem of domestic abuse is only now beginning to be addressed.

CHAPTER 6

Gender and Sexuality

Gender is an important aspect of social organization that can affect everything from day-to-day decision making within families to the distribution of men and women across the workforce. China is a particularly interesting case of gender relations because it provides a long historical record of a well-developed ideology dedicated to the oppression of women that was overthrown by an ideology dedicated to equality between the sexes. Sexuality in China is also of interest because both the Confucian and Communist ideologies tried to either repress sexual expression (especially for women) or to channel it in a few, institutionally approved directions. However, the economic reform and other recent changes in China have had important, and largely unintended, effects on sexuality, including the appearance of social scientists who are willing to study this form of human behavior.

THE HISTORY OF GENDER IN CHINA

As in most other parts of the premodern world, traditional Chinese gender roles and values started from the proposition that women should be subjugated to men. In Confucian ideology, a woman's duty was to serve her parents before she married and serve her husband and his parents after she married. The relationship between a wife and a husband was one of a subordinate to a superior, like a subject to his emperor or a son to his father. In addition, it was a wife's duty to satisfy her husband's sexual needs (Liu 1993: 123).

This is what the written record of Chinese history would have us believe; however, it is important to remember that almost all of these records were written by men, and by upper-class, middle-aged, or old men at that. There has also been a strong tendency for Chinese historians to write *didactic history,* that is, history that teaches a moral lesson. In the few cases where women are even mentioned in Chinese historical writing, the lesson was that men should hold a higher position than women. Thus, the written record of what supposedly happened to women in China may not be entirely dependable and cannot be taken at face value.

Why should we be interested in the role of women in China in traditional times? Over the past 40 years, women have made more progress in every sphere of life in China than have women in most other poor and underdeveloped nations. Whether we look at freedom of marriage and rights within marriage, levels of female education, or labor force participation and job choice, women in China enjoy more freedoms and choices than do their sisters elsewhere in the developing world.

Changing Western Views of Gender in China

The question is whether this change in gender roles is more *revolutionary* (i.e., a dramatic break with the past) or *evolutionary* (a gradual process, where the roots of current trends can be seen in the past). If a scholar was writing on gender in China in about 1970, he or she would probably have stressed the revolutionary aspect: Chinese gender relations since 1949 seemed to be almost completely different than they had been before the revolution, a vast improvement for the better.

Yet more recent analysis of the relationships between Chinese men and women suggest that the question is more complex. As foreign feminists and students of gender began to enter China to work and study during the 1970s and 1980s, they discovered that many of the supposedly revolutionary changes in gender relations were simply old Chinese gender practices in modern garb (Andors 1983, Wolf 1985). Some went so far as to describe China as a state with "patriarchal socialism," especially in rural areas (Johnson 1983; Stacey 1983). They claimed that many of the social reforms designed to benefit women ended up exploiting them, or the reforms were instituted in such a half-hearted way that the freedoms women gained existed mostly on paper (Robinson 1985). In addition, social historians and anthropologists began to see that the history of women in China was not a story of complete subjugation and oppression at all times and places; women did better in some eras than others, and customs in some areas gave women more protection and freedom than elsewhere (Wolf and Witke 1975; Watson and Ebrey 1990).

For example, during the 1930s the agricultural economist John Lossing Buck (1937) and his colleagues at Nankai University in Tianjin found that women in the wheat-growing regions of China (mostly in the north) were far less likely to work in the fields than women in the rice-growing regions of the south and west. This distinction has persisted into the 1980s; an analysis of 1982 census data shows that in both rural and urban areas, women in the south and west tended to have higher rates of labor force participation, and northern Chinese women tended to stay at home (Barrett, Bridges, Semyonov, and Gao 1991). Thus, even in the face of one of the most intense national mobilizations of women's labor force by any government, traditional cultural patterns and ideas about women's roles have persisted.

The economic reforms of the 1980s and 1990s led both Chinese and foreign feminists to question whether women were losing or gaining rights and benefits. From the late 1950s on, farm women were usually paid employees (albeit at a lower rate than men) on rural work teams and production brigades. The return to family farming in many areas of the countryside after 1978 meant that women often returned to their pre-1949 status as unpaid family laborers. Women workers in the new private sector firms and factories have few of the benefits or forms of protection that their sisters in state- or municipal-run organizations have. These changes in gender roles are under debate in China. While the revolutionary ideology that "women hold up half the sky" is still the official line, actual day-to-day practices on farms and in factories may be undermining the position of women in China.

If the position of women in China is being undermined, why is it happening and where is it leading? There are several possible answers here. One simplistic answer is that traditional gender relations are reasserting themselves. That is, once the revolutionary pressures for gender equality ease off, the unequal gender ideology of traditional Chinese culture will once again become a major organizing principle in society. However, China in the 1990s is a very different place from the prerevolutionary society: There are many advanced urban areas, and even many rural areas are tied into the networks of world markets. The kinds of gender relations found in similar Third World nations linked to the world economic system may begin to emerge in China as well.

GENDER SOCIALIZATION

Traditionally, sons received better treatment than daughters, but the rationale was not just misogyny or prejudice against women. Since daughters were expected to marry and live elsewhere, parents felt that they were, in effect, "raising daughters for someone else" and that other families would reap the benefits of their investment in a daughter.

After 1949, the Communist state tried to equalize opportunity for women for reasons of ideology and because it wanted to bring women into the labor force. The Marriage Law of 1950 (forbidding arranged and child marriages; Palmer 1995), the foundation of Women's Federations and other government organs, and the suppression of patriarchal clans and lineages all had major effects on the social position of Chinese women inside and outside of the family. The long-term effects of these changes can be seen in two key areas of gender stratification: education and employment.

Education and Gender

As was mentioned in Chapter 4, China has not been able to completely wipe out gender biases in education, and in some ways the economic reforms may have exacerbated these problems, especially at lower levels of schooling. Nationwide, only 46 percent of all primary school students in 1990 were girls (61.2 million out of 132.5 million), and only 43 percent of the nation's 34.5 million junior middle school students were female (Population Census Office 1993a: 35). Less than 40 percent of senior middle school students and 33 percent of current university students were female (Population Census Office 1993a: 33–34). Thus a smaller proportion of girls than boys attend primary schools, and the rate of attendance among female students declines rapidly at higher educational levels.

Among adult women, illiteracy and semiliteracy is a major problem; the 1990 census listed almost a third of all women age 15 or older in this category (31.9 percent, compared to 13 percent of adult men; Population Census Office 1993b: 279). Of the 127 million adult illiterate and semiliterate women, 107 million were in the countryside; one-third of all country women at age 36 and more than half at age 47 were illiterate (Population Census Office 1993b: 291–93). Male rates of illiteracy in the countryside were usually 15 to 40 percent lower than those of women; the gap widens with age. A large proportion of Chinese women in the countryside, including one out of every ten women aged 15–25, will be seriously handicapped from taking advantage of the economic boom because they cannot read or write effectively.

Gender, the Labor Force, and Occupation

In both China and the United States in 1990, 45 percent of the total labor force was female (see Table 6–1 and Anderton et al. 1997: 541). The high rate of female labor force participation makes women an important part of the Chinese economy.

The increased educational opportunities for women since 1949 have enabled them to move into nontraditional occupations. In 1990 (Table 6–1) women made up almost half of the agricultural and primary sector workforce (47.9 percent), almost half of all sales workers (46.7 percent), and more than half of all service workers (51.6 percent). They were also well-represented among the large category (almost 100 million workers) of production, transport, and related workers (35.7 percent). Only in the areas of clerical and related workers (25.6 percent) and the powerful occupational category of heads of government agencies, party committees, people's organizations, enterprises, and institutions (11.5 percent) were women poorly represented relative to their overall proportion in the workforce.

The gender composition of the Chinese occupational structure at least in these broad categories, looks fairly similar to that found in the United States; but there are several major differences. In both China and the United

TABLE 6-1

Gender Distribution of the Major Categories of the
Occupational Structure in China, 1990 (in millions)

Occupational Category	Total	Males	Females	Percent Female
Professional and technical	34.39	18.83	15.56	45.2%
Heads of government agencies*	11.33	10.02	1.30	11.5
Clerical and related workers	11.28	8.38	2.89	25.6
Sales workers	19.47	10.39	9.09	46.7
Service workers	15.51	7.50	8.01	51.6
Agriculture†	456.82	237.81	219.01	47.9
Production, transport, and related workers	98.12	63.12	35.01	35.7
Laborers not elsewhere classified	0.32	0.18	0.14	43.8
Total	647.24	356.23	291.01	45.0

*Full category name is "heads of government agencies, party committees, people's organizations, enterprises, and institutions."
† Full category name is "agriculture, animal husbandry and forestry workers, fishermen, and hunters."
Source: Population Census Office 1993a: 46–49; 1993d: 533.

States, about half of all professional and technical and sales workers are women. While women make up almost 52 percent of all service workers in China, in the United States they are 58 percent of workers in this category in 1990 (Anderton et al. 1997: 591). In the United States, only about 20 percent of all production, transport, and related workers (i.e., skilled and unskilled production workers, handlers, and transport workers) are women, compared to better than one in three (35 percent) in China.

The largest cross-national differences are in the bureaucratic sectors of the economy. In China, only one in four (25.6 percent) of all clerical workers are female; in the United States more than three in four (77 percent) are. Although in the United States the pinnacle of management is still largely male (and white), by 1990 those in the executive, administrative, and managerial occupations were 42 percent female. In China, the equivalent management category, heads of government agencies and so forth, was only 11.5 percent female.

Thus to a much greater degree than in the United States, the key organizations of government and the organs of the Communist Party have been heavily male, not just at the top, but all the way down to the clerical level. We know of no studies on this topic, but one possible conclusion is that the shift toward a market economy and the decline in employment in this sector is going to hurt men much more than it will women.

On the other hand, the greater representation of Chinese women in production, transport, and related workers than in the United States

(36 percent, compared to about 20 percent) may have the potential for greater decreases in female employment, if women are heavily concentrated in the state employment sector. It is quite difficult to get accurate data on state sector employment, but this sector is probably more heavily male than the collective or private sectors, so marketization and the disappearance of state industries may not have a major effect on women's employment. Much may depend on the levels of education and skills among displaced workers; women generally fare worse than men here. Data from a variety of sources indicate that prejudice against women workers is now more open in the private sector, and they are sometimes discriminated against in terms of hiring, salaries, sexual harassment, and discharge. Apparently, much of the discrimination against younger women workers is due to a reluctance to hire employees who may get pregnant and must be replaced at a later date.

Some occupations have a higher proportion of women in China than in the United States. For example, in 1990, 45 percent of all medical doctors in China were women (Population Census Office 1993b: 730). In the United States, only 20.7 percent of physicians were female in 1990 (Anderton et al. 1997: 601). As in other socialist nations, the medical profession is much more evenly divided between the sexes; on the other hand, doctors' incomes in these nations (relative to those of the rest of the population) tend to be considerably lower than in the United States.

SEXUALITY IN CHINA—A QUIET REVOLUTION

> Human sexuality is a diverse phenomenon. It occurs in different physical locations and social contexts, consists of a wide range of specific activities, and is perceived differently by different people.
>
> *Laumann et al. 1994: 3*

Sexuality is fundamentally shaped by social conditions and has profound consequences for society. In this section, we briefly review the sexual norms and practices in Chinese history, compare sexual attitudes and behavior in contemporary China and the United States, and discuss some of the recent trends relating to sexuality in China.

Sexuality in Traditional China

Chinese civilization has been diverse, inclusive, and fluctuating rather than monolithic, exclusive, or rigid. Sexual practices and sexual attitudes, as a central component of the traditional culture, reflected the dominant Confucian ideological system and varied from one dynasty to another to accommodate different political and social needs. The privileges that the ruling class was entitled to extended to the ways in which their sexual life was arranged, and differences in sexual practices also reflected and corresponded to the established social hierarchy. Although monogamy was codified at the beginning of the feudal society, male rulers were able to possess more women by establishing a complicated concubine system.

Throughout ancient Chinese history, the exploitation and discrimination against women was also reflected not only in the dominant view of women as servants and an inferior species but also in the prevailing treatment of women as sex objects. Such attitudes were infused in the widespread practice of acquiring concubines (minor wives), the long-lasting system of prostitution, and the standards of beauty that often subjected women to physical and mental suffering.

Most emperors had thousands or tens of thousands of young women in their palaces to provide various services, including sexual ones. Among the ruling class, status differentiation also determined the appropriate sexual arrangements, and the number of women a man could own was often a symbol of power and wealth. The ruling class often prohibited any marital relationship across class lines or the promotion of a concubine to the status of the wife (Liu 1993: 269, 441).

The entire Chinese dynastic system was built on political, economic, and ideological centralization; sexual repression became an essential part of political and social control, especially during periods of crisis. The basic requirements were that married women be restricted to their homes and not come in contract with any men other than their husbands (Liu 1993: 591). Although a man could maintain sexual relationships with many women at the same time, chastity was an important female virtue; a woman could only belong to one man in her lifetime (Liu 1993: 243–47). Female chastity was valued over life, and Confucian moralists wrote many tales about the extremes to which wives and virtuous widows would go (including suicide) to prevent even the appearance of immoral behavior. "The traditional words for virginity, *zhenjie*, and for a virgin, *chunu*, both refer only to a female" (Kristof and WuDunn 1994: 298).

The most dehumanizing practice was foot-binding. Early in Chinese history, women with small feet were considered sexually attractive. During the tenth century AD (the Song dynasty; see Table 1–1) it became a custom for women to keep their feet small by forcing female children to bind them using cloth. Small feet were such a status symbol that ordinary families were willing to bind the feet of their female family members, which involved breaking and deforming the bones of the foot, starting at the age of four or five. This practice was also imposed by the male-centered culture that catered to this peculiar erotic taste. Undoubtedly, foot-binding often had devastating health consequences in addition to physical pain. This custom spread from the upper to the lower classes; in many areas of China in the early twentieth century at least 60–70 percent of all adult women had bound feet.

Sexuality in Twentieth-Century China

During the first half of the twentieth century, there were slow changes in sexuality in China, especially in the larger cities. Foot-binding gradually disappeared during the first half of the twentieth century, partially due to anti–foot-binding societies that sprang up throughout China. Women, and sometimes men, found that they could escape a loveless or abusive marriage by escaping to the new and growing cities. However, the lack of enforcement of new laws protecting women in many areas of China, especially in the countryside, the power of criminal gangs to control prostitution and drugs, and the fact that many women lived on the edge of starvation meant that their position had changed little from that of women during the Qing dynasty.

The Communist Party saw that the emancipation of women could be an important part of class struggle in China. Four fundamental changes took place when the People's Republic was established in 1949. The first was the elimination of slavery, the selling of women and children. The second was the complete elimination of prostitution and the gangs that controlled it. The third was true, legally defined and enforced monogamy and government support for young women against oppression by their husbands and parents-in-law. The fourth was prohibition of "unhealthy and superstitious practices" resulting in harm to women, including fortune-telling and the use of ineffective traditional medicines (Pan 1995: 65). Various efforts were made to realize Mao's statement that "women can hold up half of the sky." However, as Chinese society became more and more politicized in the 1960s and 1970s, the subject of sex was increasingly in conflict with Communist ideology and had to be ignored and suppressed.

Communist Asceticism

Since the entire socialist system was built on the political polarization of the revolutionary and pure proletarian class versus the reactionary and decadent capitalist class, any sexual expression was associated with an immoral capitalist lifestyle. As George Orwell had shown in his antiutopian novel *1984* (published in 1948), totalitarian regimes found sexuality to be intolerable not because it offended morality, but rather because it was an expression of individualism. Sexuality was a potential conspiracy of two or more individuals directed toward an unsanctioned goal. In China, sexual suppression through more than two decades was best reflected in the strict media control and the absence of any sexual topics in literary works.

Based on the principle that literature and art must serve the need of politics and class struggle, sexual expression and love stories, which were common themes in traditional Chinese novels and poetry, disappeared. The new heroes and heroines of stories, novels, plays, and "revolutionary operas" were completely devoted to the revolutionary cause and did not have family members or normal human emotions to complicate the story. Only the stereotypical bad guys might have sexual needs, and not much description was allowed here, either.

During the Cultural Revolution (1966–68; Table 3–1), Chinese society became virtually sexless; anything related to sex became taboo. Makeup vanished, clothing became uniform and almost unisex, and men and women were supposed to pick marriage partners on the basis of revolutionary fervor and class background, not romantic attraction. The dictionaries published during this period did not even include words such as *prostitute* or *sexual intercourse.*

Numerous anecdotes show how this asceticism produced stupidity. In one case, the groom promised his father-in-law that he would not have sex with his daughter because that was a "capitalist lifestyle" (Pan 1995: 69). One of the lasting impacts of sexual suppression was the lack of sex education. Even today in China, young people receive little or no sex education or preparation for childbirth. Yet making people believe that childbirth is a mysterious, dangerous, and painful process may help support the goals of the One-Child Policy (this is what sociologists refer to as a latent function).

Sexual repression and stupidity did not eliminate criminal sexual offenses or the underground circulation of pornographic materials. Organized sex crimes persisted in many cities even though rape is a capital offense. Rape is probably even more heavily underreported in China than in Western nations because of the traditional view that women have a duty to keep their chastity regardless of the circumstances.

During this era (1966–76), the mass media did not encourage young people to think about sex or love. Instead, there was a constant drumbeat of propaganda (often through loudspeakers booming throughout the village or neighborhood) about self-sacrifice for the party and the new China. Youth with an interest in the opposite sex were handicapped by sex-segregated schools, and lots of nosy neighbors, teachers, and party members looked for young people who might be expressing their bourgeois individualism in such an unhealthy way. In some senses, the pre-1949 system of social control of young people, especially girls, was shifted from benefiting parents and kin to benefiting the party and the state.

State campaigns against early marriage, which began to be enforced nationwide from about 1972 on (Parish and Whyte 1978: 162), represent another aspect of sexual repression. By the early 1970s, the median age at marriage was about 28 years for men and 24 years for women; rural marriage ages were usually about three to four years younger for each sex (Parish and Whyte, 1978: 163; Whyte and Parish 1984: 113). In a society with very strong rules against premarital sexual activity and especially against premarital pregnancy (contraceptives would not be provided for unmarried men and women), increasing the marriage age also meant preventing sexual activity well into the mid-20s.

After 1978, this system of control of young people began to break down. Love ballads and rock and roll began to be smuggled in from Hong Kong, Taiwan, and the West, and old and new novels about love and romance found favor among young people. Young couples in cities began to find some degree of privacy in public parks after dark. They began to take an interest in fashion, especially when they would no longer be punished for wearing attractive clothes or makeup. Western-style advertisements, movie-star magazines, and other aspects of youth culture led to new perceptions of the self and of potential mates. This slow change in sexual mores took place throughout the 1980s and 1990s. China is still, especially in rural areas, one of the world's more conservative societies, but change took place at the margins.

SEXUAL ATTITUDES AND PRACTICE: SOME COMPARATIVE NUMBERS

Recent surveys on sexual practices and attitudes in China and some Western countries make possible empirical comparisons of sexual behavior across different cultures and systems. Despite some differences in method and timing, the results from the Chinese Sex Civilization Survey (Liu 1992)[1] and the U.S. National Health and Social Life Survey (Laumann et al. 1994) can be used to compare sexual practices and attitudes in China and the United States.

There is a much stronger normative pressure against premarital sex in China than in the United States. According to the U.S. survey, 57 percent of men and 46 percent of women had their first sexual experience before age 18, and about 10 percent of men and 22 percent of women reported having the first sexual experience with their spouse (Laumann et al. 1994: 324, 331). In the Chinese sample of married couples, 6 percent of the respondents in the cities and 18 percent of those in the countryside reported having their first sexual experience before age 20; almost none would have been married at that time. More than 91 percent of men and 96 percent of women reported having their first sexual experience with their future spouse (Liu 1992: 317). Chinese society is not as puritanical as it is sometimes presented, but premarital sex (which is three times more common in the countryside than in the cities) appears to be usually just that: sexual relations between a couple who have a strong commitment to marry in the future.

---

[1] Chinese scholars have responded to these changes with several important studies. *Sexual Behavior in Modern China* (1992), written by Liu (a sociologist from Shanghai), is sometimes called the Kinsey Report of China. With data for 28 regions in 15 provinces, it includes information on adolescent sexuality, source of sexual knowledge and beliefs, sexual crimes, STDs, marital discord, and premarital and extramarital sexual incidence and attitudes. Those findings cannot be generalized to the population at large because its sampling frame relied heavily on opportunistic samples (pp. 23–26). There were three special samples of middle school students, college students, and prisoners, all of whom provided information on critical subgroups. There was also a sample of 7,602 currently married individuals. It is possible that there is more underreporting of illegal sex acts in the Chinese survey because of the harsher penalties that could result from such an admission.

Sexual Activity among Chinese and Americans

In general, Americans tend to start having sex at a younger age and accumulate a higher number of sex partners than Chinese people. Chinese youth report that they were much less sexually active than their American counterparts, currently or in the past 12 months. About half the college students in China did not have a sex partner in the last year, compared to only 11 percent of Americans aged 18 to 24. Among the sexually active, the Chinese youth were much less likely to have multiple sex partners than Americans. Only 18 percent of Chinese male and 11 percent of female college students had two or more sex partners in the last year, compared to a third of all American youth aged 18–24 (Liu 1992: 191,504; Laumann et al. 1994: 177).

After marriage, however, the Chinese and the Americans became more similar in terms of the number of sex partners in the past 12 months or currently, and American males were less prone to have extramarital relations than were their Chinese counterparts. More than 90 percent of married men and women in both countries did not report having extramarital sexual relationships. Yet the married Chinese reported a higher rate (10 percent of men, 4 percent of women) of multiple partners after marriage compared to Americans (4 percent for men and women). This is probably related to a greater propensity among Americans to divorce if they find another sexual partner. Divorce, and finding housing after divorce, is still not an easy process in China (Palmer 1995). Many Chinese married couples suffer from long-distance separation by work assignments, whether by choice or accident. These separations can often lead to extramarital affairs.

Frequency of Sexual Relations

American couples seem to have sex more often than Chinese couples. About 43 percent of married Americans report having sex "a few times a week" or "almost everyday"; the figures for China are 40 percent for rural respondents and 29 percent for urban ones (Liu 1992: 337; Laumann et al. 1994: 88). There are several plausible explanations for this. The cultural explanation is that Americans live in a society that puts great emphasis on sexual fulfillment for both men and women. Another explanation for a lower frequency of intercourse is the Chinese folk belief that having frequent sex is detrimental to a man's health. It is widely believed in China that "one drop of sperm is as precious as ten drops of blood." In addition, Chinese sexual mores often discourage women from initiating lovemaking.

A simpler explanation for the differences in sexual frequency between Americans and rural and urban Chinese is that in most Chinese cities, residential housing is still tight: Married couples often have to share a bedroom with their children or parents. Married couples in urban China often find few opportunities for moments of intimacy. Housing is less of a problem in villages, which may be one reason rural couples seem to have sex more often than urban couples.

RECENT CHANGES IN SEXUAL ATTITUDES AND BEHAVIOR

As with many other aspects of Chinese society, sexual attitudes and sexual behavior have changed dramatically since the end of the Maoist era in the late 1970s. Chinese society has recently experienced striking changes in people's perceptions of, attitudes toward, and behavior relating to sexuality. Some most noticeable trends include (1) sexual behavior is separated from procreation; (2) women are better able to express their needs; (3) sexual practices are becoming more diverse; (4) premarital sex has became more acceptable; (5) extramarital sex is more common; (5) the divorce rate is rising; (6) sex crimes are more serious; and (7) prostitution is growing rapidly (Liu 1992: 12; Pan 1995: 519–23).

In one survey among those married before 1958, 12 percent of the respondents reported started having sex before marriage. This proportion increased to 81 percent among those who got married after 1979 (Pan 1995: 524). Most of the premarital sex happened between couples who later married. In another survey, only 11 percent of the female respondents reported that the purpose of having sex was to have a child, whereas 41 percent reported that they wanted to achieve orgasm more frequently (Pan 1995: 519).

There have also been a few studies on homosexuality in China. According to Pan, a sociologist and sexologist, homosexuals should feel freer than their Western counterparts. This is not because homosexuality is more accepted in China, but because most people are not aware of it. People of the same gender can share a hotel room, but for a man and a woman to check in, a marriage license is often required. On the other hand, since homosexuality is not acceptable or even perceivable to many Chinese, some gay men are married and have families even though they have male sex partners and consider themselves gay. However, it is more difficult to develop and maintain a stable or openly homosexual relationship. The decline in social control in China's large cities, the growth of a commercialized sex industry, and the increasing anonymity of urban life may make it easier for a covert homosexual subculture to emerge there.

The Sex Industry

In the early 1970s, when asked by a foreign reporter about whether there were still prostitutes in China, the late Chinese premier Zhou Enlai said, "Yes, in Taiwan." The Communist government did achieve the objective of eliminating prostitution in mainland China from the 1950s through the early 1970s (Henriot 1995). However, prostitution reappeared in the late 1970s and early 1980s in the new **Special Economic Zones** and became a widespread phenomenon in the 1990s. Nationwide, 25,021 were arrested for engaging in prostitution in 1986. The number increased to 50,822 in 1988 and 137,000 in 1990. According to police estimates, only 10 to 20 percent of all those engaged in prostitution were actually arrested (Shan 1995: 379).

At the social level, the rural-urban dichotomy, poverty, unequal distribution of wealth, lack of social control, and discrimination against women all contributed to the reemergence of prostitution in China. The poverty and lack of social mobility in backward rural areas pushed many women to search for opportunities in large cities and coastal regions. Some were lured while others were forced to become prostitutes when other chances of making a decent living were limited. At the same time, some of those who acquired a large amount of money overnight constitute the demand side of prostitution.

The evaporation of the Marxist belief system in China during the reform period left an ideological vacuum, resulting in the weakening of social control. Social morality and order were often traded for economic gains. On the one hand, local government and the police did not have much incentive to crack down on prostitution when it was believed to promote tourism and generate more tax money. On the other hand, moral standards were challenged among ordinary people when money became the primary concern of life. Massive migration further weakened traditional social control by the community and family.

Deeply rooted gender discrimination has often prevented women from getting comparable education or job opportunities as men. Some women are the object of sexual harassment or abuse by private employers. Many young rural women who move to a new area to work but who have been raped, sexually abused, or seduced know that it will be difficult to find a husband at home, and prostitution often looks like the only way out. In some rural marriage arrangements, women are treated as private property that can be bought, sold, or traded. One type of organized crime is women-trafficking—forcing women to become prostitutes or selling kidnapped women to men in distant regions, often men in poor villages who have almost no other means of getting women to move there (Kristof and WuDunn 1994 : 212–22).

Sexually Transmitted Diseases (STDs)

Along with the evidence of liberalization of sexual practices, there are early warnings of a growing risk of an STD epidemic in China resulting from a faltering government campaign against widespread prostitution, a weakening of ideological and moral restraints, and a population that has little knowledge of strategies for preventing the spread of STDs. It is generally held that the actual number of cases of sexually transmitted diseases is several times that reported.

More important, the incidence of STDs has been increasing at the rate of 47 percent per year in the adult population since 1980, and 77 percent per year among children under 14 since 1987, most of whom acquired the disease from a parent. The World Health Organization (WHO) predicts that by the year 2000 China will have 200,000 cases of HIV infection, which is double the number predicted by the Chinese government (*People's Daily* December 3, 1994: 1). Studies have also suggested that STD incidence rates were highest among people in their 20s to 40s and among less-educated people and traveling businesspersons.

Realizing the seriousness of the problem, the Chinese government has begun to collaborate with international organizations in an effort to control the rapidly increasing incidence of STDs. The World Bank, the World Health Organization, the United Nations Development Program (UNDP), the United Nations International Children's Emergency Fund (UNICEF), the Australian government, and some other international and national organizations have begun to provide funds, equipment, and medical and technical assistance to help control the spread of STDs in China.

Geographically, AIDS appears to be most common in larger cities and in southern areas like Yunnan province, the home of many young Chinese women who have spent time in Thailand (a nation with the highest rate of AIDS in Asia) as prostitutes. The recent spread of drug addiction, and especially intravenous drug use, in China may be another avenue for AIDS infection. Since there is little HIV testing of blood and blood products used for transfusions in China, this possible route of AIDS transmission (which was important in Western nations and Japan from the late 1970s to the mid-1980s) may be a significant challenge for China as well.

Hepatitis B, which can cause early death from liver cancer, is also endemic in China and can be spread in the same ways as HIV. Only about a third of Chinese infants are immunized against it, and there is virtually no attempt to immunize adolescents or adults. The combination of the reemergence of prostitution and the large-scale migration of young people has the potential to spread this disease even more widely across China.

SUMMARY

Social differentiation by gender is found in every society. Traditional Chinese society was perhaps unique in the extent of its philosophical justification of the domination of men over women, which was not always successful in practice. The Communist Party made the overthrow of the Confucian system of gender one of its primary goals.

When examined on the dimensions of education and occupation, this bold attempt to overthrow several millennia of gender exploitation has fallen short of perfection, but China compares well with most other Third World nations in this regard. Rural female illiteracy is still a major problem, and women are less well represented at higher levels of education. Just as in the United States, 45 percent of China's workforce is female. Their distribution across the occupational spectrum is similar to that found in the United States, except for managerial positions in the government and Communist Party, where they account for only about one position out of every ten.

Throughout the traditional period, sexuality and gender relationships were governed by the principle of male superiority and female inferiority. During the first three decades of the Communist regime, female exploitation was legally prohibited. At the same time, sex became virtually taboo and the entire society was politicized and largely sexless.

In recent years, fundamental changes have taken place in China regarding sexual practices and attitudes; a quiet sexual revolution seems to be underway. On the one hand, sex is no longer a taboo, and it is more acceptable for people, especially women, to express their concerns and needs related to their sexual activities. On the other hand, there is also a rise in sex crimes, prostitution, and other forms of exchange using sexual favors from women as a commodity. Sexually transmitted diseases are also on the rise as a result of inadequate public health services (especially sex education), the revival of prostitution, and ignorance.

CHAPTER 7

Work

WORK IN TRADITIONAL CHINA

In traditional China, at least four out of five workers were farmers. They usually worked on small farms; in only a few places did large-scale managerial estates employ many workers. Many of these farmers were full tenants, who owned no land and had to rent from year to year. Others were part-owners and part-tenants, meaning that they owned insufficient land to live on and had to rent more. These farmers had to pay their rent in many different ways in various parts of China: in cash, in a fixed amount of their crop, in share contracts, and so on (Tawney 1932; Barrett 1984).

A sizable proportion of the agricultural population were farmers who owned and farmed their own land. A much smaller portion of the population, no more than 5–10 percent, were landlords and their dependents. The landlord class did no physical labor; they lived primarily on rent from land leased to tenants, from loan-sharking, and from pawnbrokering. Finally, about 5–10 percent of the rural workforce were landless laborers, who often had to eke out a living by moving from place to place and selling their labor, either on a daily or seasonal basis.

While there were great differences in wealth in traditional rural China, there was also a significant amount of social mobility. Families could go from poverty to wealth in the space of a generation or two, as in Pearl Buck's novel *The Good Earth*. On the other hand, bad weather, family calamity, bad politics, or the three classic addictions of young men in prerevolutionary China—gambling, prostitutes, and opium—could dissipate a family fortune in short order.

At the bottom of the occupational ladder were those who teetered on the edge of starvation: agricultural laborers, casual laborers in cities, thieves, bandits, streetwalkers, and so on. In an overpopulated nation like China, this group was constantly being replenished by those pushed to the margin of existence by various misfortunes.

Most of the remaining traditional workforce was employed in handicraft production, such as those who wove silk or bamboo baskets; in natural resource exploitation, such as fishermen or charcoal-burners; or as service personnel to the upper classes or to the government, such as clerks, bailiffs, soldiers, and employees of inns, restaurants, and brothels. While some of these occupations had rules against easy entry by outsiders (such as urban guilds), China had few laws restricting social mobility between occupations. In fact, the ups and downs of the market, relatively easy migration, and the competitive imperial examination system all tended to result in some degree of inter- and intragenerational occupational mobility.

For most Chinese in the traditional era, the household was a unit of kinship, consumption, and production. Family members turned over most or all of their paychecks (if they had outside income) to the household head, who would frequently try to economize as much as possible on daily consumption activities. Many Chinese farm families ate meat only a few times a year; meals would frequently be only rice, sweet potatoes, or noodles flavored with a few cooked vegetables. Close kin were coworkers, and decisions about marriage and coresidence often were heavily influenced by concerns about family prosperity and sometimes even family survival.

EFFECTS OF THE COMMUNIST REVOLUTION

After decades of violent war and chaos, and facing international isolation as a result of the containment foreign policy of the United States during the Cold War period, the new government established by the Chinese Communist Party in 1949 committed itself to pursue two basic, but sometimes competing, economic objectives. The first was to quickly transform China into an industrial nation. The second was to create and maintain social equality among all citizens. To achieve the first objective, the Communist government established a Stalinist-type state: a centralized economic system characterized by state ownership of the means of production, and bureaucratic, rather than market-driven, allocation of resources. To achieve the second objective, the ruling party monopolized the channels of mobility and demanded political conformity (see Chapter 3) and economic sacrifice from all the people.

According to Kornai's "main line of causality," the key foci of Communist states are the undivided power of the party and the domination of its ideology (1992). The party has a right to dominate in all social spheres, and state ownership is the only legitimate form of property right. These two fundamental features then lead to the dominance of bureaucratic coordination (such as five-year plans) and the elimination of market mechanisms. Besides ideological imperatives, the political leaders were also driven by a desire to accumulate state capital, generate economic growth, and achieve industrialization. As a result, sectors such as energy, transportation, steel and iron, and heavy machinery were favored by state planning and budget agencies for generous allocation of resources and incentives (Bian 1994). Such development strategies also resulted in workplace segmentation, which shaped the patterns of mobility and inequality in China.

The economic role of a state-owned enterprise is limited in the absence of markets. Capital investments and raw materials were provided through the administrative allocation system. Leaders were appointed by the party. The workforce was channeled through the state or local labor bureaus. The outputs were also distributed by the state (Kaple, 1994). As a result, the enterprise and the state formed a bargaining relationship.

The Work Unit

What has been unique about socialist enterprises in general, and the pre-reform Chinese enterprises in particular, was that they performed most of the social functions that are usually the responsibilities of other organizations or institutions in other societies. Instead of exchanging a payment for the productive activities on the part of the workers, the enterprise is responsible for the workers' lives.

This economic system had an entirely different logic from the one that previously prevailed. People were organized into **work units,** or **danwei,** (pronounced dahn-way), that had no relationship to their family's status. In many respects, the work unit was designed to take the place of kinship ties. It assigned work, set hours and levels of compensation, and provided housing, medical care, and consumer goods. Few if any decisions were left to either the individual worker or the family unit of which he or she was a part.

Rural and urban work units were also designed to mobilize women workers (Barrett et al. 1991). Day care and other needed services were provided, and organizations such as the Women's Federation encouraged women to engage in paid labor. Since paid labor service also became linked to obtaining work points or ration coupons, and with them the possibility of obtaining consumer durables, there were even more reasons for families to reorganize their schedules so that women could work outside the home.

New Work Organizations in Rural Areas

In the countryside, farm workers in the 1950s became part of **production teams** usually made up of several dozen workers (see Chapter 3), which in turn were part of **production brigades,** made up of several hundred workers and roughly equivalent to the pre-1949 natural village. Depending upon the era, farm workers would be rewarded according to their contribution, measured in work points, to the overall production goals achieved by their production team or brigade. Decisions about workforce allocation and reward had been shifted far above the level of the individual farmer. About the only unit of production directly under the control of the farm worker was the private plot, a small garden allotted to each family. Yet while the sum of all workers' private plots was seldom more than about 5 percent of the work unit's land, they were an important source of vegetables, and when rural markets were permitted, they were a source of cash income as well.

URBAN EMPLOYMENT PRACTICES BEFORE REFORM (PRE-1979)

Urban employment practices reflected both the political selection by the government labor bureaus and personal influence of the job seekers. Job assignments were handled by labor bureaus at various government levels with little consideration of individuals' desires. During the Cultural Revolution, many scientists and engineers were sent to remote areas to develop nuclear weapons and space technology. Tens of millions of urban youth were sent to the countryside to work on the land. However, recent studies have found that power, personal influence, and informal social connections have largely eroded the bureaucratic process of job allocation (Bian 1994: 122).

Employment was customarily for life; the enterprise was expected to provide adequate housing and free health care to all of its employees. Extended absence from work was usually permitted for health or family reasons with full salary payments. All workers were entitled to a pension after retirement. In addition, a state-owned enterprise often provided its employees with free child-care services, subsidized meal services, and free vocational training for the employees' children.

Not only did the employees work in the same factory, they also lived together in the same apartment compound and went to the same places for shopping, recreation, and other social activities. The lack of a labor market limited job mobility. An underdeveloped transportation system also discouraged family members from working in different enterprises due to commuting problems. As a result, during the first three decades of the Communist regime, a state enterprise in China became like a big family or a small society, relatively self-sufficient and insulated. The workplace provided a major source of community and identity.

Since the workplace was responsible for a worker in most aspects of his or her daily life for his or her entire lifetime, and because job mobility was minimal, stratification and inequality among workers were determined by the stratification or segmentation of different workplaces. Employees from large state enterprises with high administrative rank were able to receive better housing, medical care, and child care and more benefits than employees from lower-ranking state

enterprises. State sector workers in general were entitled to greater rewards than collective sector workers. In addition, social identity was
more attached to the workplace than to occupation or region. Instead
of asking "What do you do?" most people asked "Which work unit are
you from?" to start a conversation or to try to estimate someone's social and economic standing.

SOCIALIST ECONOMIC REFORMS—IN THEORY

"The rise of bureaucracy is a worldwide movement, but Communist systems push it further than in any other systems" (Lindblom 1977: 239),
leading to problems of information overload, misprioritization, inefficient factor allocation, inadequate technology, conflict of incentives, and
failures of national planning (Ellman 1989). More specifically, the actual
behavior of economic planning and bargaining at the state, ministerial,
regional, and firm levels resulted in a drive toward quantity at the expense of quality. Paternalism and corruption in state enterprises in-
evitably led to chronic shortages, suppressed consumption, lack of incentives, and gross inefficiency. Eventually, serious inflation, external debt,
and erosion of official ideology led to systemwide crises (Kornai 1992).

Though there is a consensus about the problems of socialism and
their causes, the proposed solutions are drastically different. Two opposing views have been suggested. One sees no compromise between
planned and market economic systems; it claims that the only viable solution is a shock therapy, or sweeping privatization and marketization.
The other view insists that gradual economic reform is not only feasible
but also desirable.

Proponents of radical changes are convinced that a mixed economic
system, combining the advantages of both socialist redistributive and
capitalist market arrangements, is just an illusion and is more likely to
create a nightmare that combines the problems of both systems. This
view holds that the socialist system is internally coherent and tends to resist piecemeal changes or reforms in any one element of the system. True
political liberalization cannot be achieved under the control of any Communist Party and its monopoly of power. Finally, partial price reforms
are unable to lead to a rational, market-based system of prices.

On the other hand, proponents of a mixed economy and gradual reform emphasize the complementarity between socialist planning and
capitalist market coordination mechanisms. Szelényi (1989) argues that
the introduction of some market measures into the stagnant socialist
economy will solve many of its problems. Naughton suggests that a
"gradual and tentative strategy of reform" is more desirable because it
allows individuals and organizations to better adapt to the changing environment, obtaining a "virtuous cycle" by strengthening the organizations' willingness and capacity to adapt, prior to the creation of full-
fledged market institutions (1995: 10).

SOCIALIST ECONOMIC REFORMS—IN CHINA

China's approach to economic reforms has been characterized as tentative, partial, and inconsistent. However, the Chinese economic reform strategy contains some coherence (Naughton 1995) and, in the past 18 years, has resulted in spectacular economic growth. China's soaring national economy, based on gradual reforms, not only adds enormous validity to the mixed-economy model of economic reforms in former socialist states, it also has stimulated research on the mechanisms of change in China. The distinctive pattern of the Chinese reform lies in its ability to achieve an after-the-fact coherence in a process of gradually "growing out of the plan" and reaching the goal of a full-fledged market economy, which the "big bang" approach is intended to achieve (Naughton 1995: 7–13).

Walder recently suggested that the behavior of the government as owner of public enterprises varies widely across government jurisdictions. Often, local governments are willing and able to control the enterprises under their jurisdiction and "manage the public industry as a diversified market-oriented firm" (1995: 263). In addition, Naughton finds that "Chinese economic policy since 1949 has been founded on the government's monopoly control of industry and the price system, which was used to pump resources into government industrialization programs. Economic reforms since 1978 have substantially weakened the government's monopoly, shrinking government fiscal resources while stimulating growth of the non-state sector" (1992: 16).

MARKETIZATION AND PRIVATIZATION, CHINESE-STYLE

Theoretical debates aside, the Chinese approach to economic reforms indeed brought encouraging changes. In contrast with the former socialist states of Eastern Europe, which have experienced severe economic recessions, China, with a private economic sector emerging from the ground up, has been among the world's fastest-growing economies since the late 1970s (see Chapter 1).

In China, industry[1] and commerce (including the wholesale, retail, and restaurant sectors) produced 41 percent and 9 percent, respectively, of the country's GDP in 1994 and have been the two most dynamic sectors, growing at an average annual rate of 15 percent and 9 percent from

---

[1] According to the China's official classification, industry, as opposed to agriculture, transportation, construction, commerce, and service sectors, refers to material production, including extraction and processing of natural resources as well as manufacturing and repairing of industrial products. Gross output value of industry (GOVI) is "the total volume of industrial products sold or available for sale in value terms which reflects the total achievements and overall scale of industrial production during a given period" (State Statistical Bureau 1995a: 422–23).

1978 to 1994 (State Statistical Bureau 1995a: 23, 25–6). They are also the two sectors that have experienced the phenomenal expansion of privately owned business. While small private manufacturers are expected to rely on technology-transfer and subcontracting opportunities from larger public enterprises, which still dominate the manufacturing sector, entrepreneurs running retail shops and restaurants in the service sector have gained a decisive advantage over publicly owned services.

Though industrial output from state enterprises increased almost seven times with an annual growth rate of more than 8 percent in the past 15 years, its share in the gross national industrial output decreased from 76 percent in 1980 to 34 percent in 1994 (State Statistical Bureau 1995a: 377). During the same period, collectively owned industry grew more than 26 times with an annual growth rate of almost 24 percent and constituted more than two-fifths of the total gross output of value of industry by 1994. As the fastest-growing sector in China, privately owned industry grew at an average annual rate of almost 140 percent in the past 15 years; its share in the national industrial output increased from zero to 12 percent during the same period.

The service sector has been dominated by private entrepreneurs in recent years, particularly in retail and restaurant sectors. In 1980, for each private retailer, there were three public (state plus collective) distributors; but by 1994, for each public distributor, there were 12 private retailers (State Statistical Bureau 1992: 584; State Statistical Bureau 1995a: 514). After 1985, there has been a steady decline in the absolute number of publicly owned retailers, many of which either were closed or went into private hands. In terms of the relative size of the workforce in the retail industry, there has been a gradual transition (gradual according to the shock therapy standard) of the retail industry from a public sector before 1980 to a private domain by 1994.[2]

The restaurant sector has experienced a similar trend. Among the 0.3 million restaurants in China in 1980, about half were privately owned. But by 1994, more than 95 percent of the 2.2 million restaurants were in private hands. Among the 1.1 million people employed in the restaurant industry in 1980, nine out of ten were grumpy state employees. But among the 6.3 million people working at restaurants in 1994, four out of five were entrepreneurs or their employees, eager to serve their customers in order to survive in a highly competitive market.

---

[2] Since more than half of the 143,000 outlets and 83 percent of the 11 million workforce in the wholesale sector still remained public in 1994 (State Statistical Bureau 1995a: 510–11), frequent private-public interactions are expected, involving both market and nonmarket, legal and quasi-legal exchanges.

WORKPLACE-CENTERED POLITICAL, ECONOMIC, AND SOCIAL LIFE

The changes in China's workplace are constant. Three central elements defined work and the workplace during Mao's era (i.e., pre-1978). First, the workplace was segmented along an ownership hierarchy. Second, the workplace performed a variety of noneconomic functions and provided a sense of community. Third, jobs were bureaucratically allocated by the labor administrations, assuring permanent employment.

Many have observed that a Chinese state enterprise is not only or even primarily an economic entity. It is, or at least has been, a relatively insulated community or small self-sufficient society. Most important, it is a political organization, entrenched by the party apparatus. Participation in various political movements and activities were given priority over economic production. To mobilize the workers effectively for political campaigns and to control the masses, the party committee was given the utmost authority at a workplace. In other words, a party secretary of a factory had more power than the factory director. At the middle management level, a party branch ensured total control by the party. The importance of both government agencies and state enterprises in China is huge, and, paradoxically, has even increased under reform policies as pressures to generate money have increased. A dry-cleaning establishment and a bakery in Beijing are both run by the State Security Bureau, the "Army General Staff Department is part owner of one of China's best hotels, the Palace, and for a time a local army unit ran a travel service that operated a brothel" (Kristof and WuDunn 1995: 346).

More than 100 million workers are employed by all branches of the government and Communist Party apparatus, roughly a third of all nonagricultural workers; 107 million workers work in other state enterprises (*Chicago Tribune* March 6, 1998). Although the Communist Party has announced plans to cut the size of government institutions by 4 million workers over the next three years, this may be a difficult task. Since these state enterprise workers are among the regime's strongest supporters in terms of ideology, the government runs considerable risks in trying to move from shrinking state enterprises through attrition to actually firing workers.

The Changing Workplace during the Reform Period

During the economic reform period, all types of industrial organizations had to engage in market competition, and ownership segmentation was reduced. Firms became more profit-oriented and gradually gave up their noneconomic obligations. These changes were intended to create new types of industrial enterprises that were fairly independent of the government.

In this new economic landscape, foreign companies and private businesses were able to offer higher salaries. Increased market competition forced many state enterprises to cut costs by reducing benefit programs and hiring more contract workers. Workplace solidarity and identity were further reduced when job security was threatened; many workers began to hold second jobs after work. The emergence of a labor market greatly facilitated job mobility and gradually transformed more industrial enterprises into open systems.

One way to reduce social overhead cost was to eliminate permanent employment and offer fewer benefit programs. Just as in many downsizing American industries, hiring contract workers became an attractive alternative for many state enterprises. The percentage of contract workers steadily increased from 8 percent in 1984 to 26 percent in 1990 and approached 50 percent in 1994 (State Statistical Bureau 1995a: 99). Although contract labor had been common in Chinese industry before 1978 (Walder 1986: 39–56), it had been mostly limited to rural workers who came in to work in urban industries. Now the concept was applied to a broader spectrum of society, including urban residents.

The Declining Significance of Ownership

The emergence of markets brings economic vitality and organizational innovation. Now, the state and collective sectors also include joint ventures of public enterprises with multinational corporations. The private sector also includes firms funded by foreign and Overseas Chinese investments. Recently, more and more state-owned enterprises have become stock companies whose shares are traded on the stock market (*The Wall Street Journal* June 1, 1998). At the same time, there was a variety of public-private partnerships and joint-venture type of economic entities. In addition, many private firms were still registered as collective enterprises to avoid political risks. All of these situations make the old state-collective-private characterization of economic entities more and more inaccurate and insignificant.

Erosion of Workplace Segmentation

Market reforms provided new opportunities for mobility and advancement, especially for those disadvantaged under the old system (see Chapter 10). Market competition is gradually replacing workplace segmentation as a major factor in social stratification and economic inequality. Recent statistics show that the income gap is widening in favor of those engaged in private or other nonstate sector employment. Many workers of the money-losing and debt-ridden state enterprises were unable to receive wages for months at a time and had to find second jobs to support themselves and their families. Some of them have given up their state jobs to work for foreign companies or engage in entrepreneurial activities. Recent survey results show that state sector workers had the lowest morale and job satisfaction in China. After 1980, the government gradually released its monopoly control over labor allocation and allowed people to find jobs on their own or become self-employed. There were 24,560 employment service agencies in 1994, playing a major role in an emerging labor market (Jiang, Lu, and Dan 1995: 126). More jobs were being created in the non-state sector than in the state sector.

SUMMARY

After 1949, gigantic state-owned and quasi-state-owned enterprises were established to not only replace the small-scale workshops and factories but also to form a community and take over many of the functions of other major social institutions and organizations during the first three decades of the Communist regime. Economic reforms of the past two decades, however, have tried to rebuild these large enterprises as economic entities with limited social responsibility, and the workers' sense of workplace identity and community has eroded.

Second, alongside the emergence of large-scale, state-owned enterprises, the socialist system created an urban working class entitled to permanent employment, free housing, medical and child care, subsidized urban living, and other fringe benefits. Yet the post-1978 economic changes have threatened the source of these entitlements and made the position of the urban working class less enviable in comparison with the emerging professionals and entrepreneurs in the thriving private sector.

In prereform China, all nonfarm jobs were allocated through the central and local labor administration bureaus, although favoritism and social connections played a significant role in getting desirable positions. Uneven economic growth has created new occupational opportunities and resulted in disgruntled employees in the state sector. At the same time, one major change during the past two decades of reforms was the collapse of the **Bamboo Wall** that prohibited rural-urban migration. As a result, a more national labor market has gradually been emerging.

CHAPTER 8

Life in Chinese Cities

[Chinese] cities had apparently not grown much in relative terms in spite of considerable economic development, slums and squatter settlements seemed absent, conspicuous consumption and foreign-oriented life styles were not visible, a high degree of economic equality and security seemed to prevail, unemployment seemed absent, close-knit neighborhoods and families seemed to persist, and crime, drug addiction, prostitution, and other forms of deviance seemed minor or nonexistent.

Whyte and Parish 1984: 2–3

For people who were living in or observing Chinese cities during the 1960s and 1970s, the above description bore many elements of truth. But for urban residents of or travelers to Chinese cities today, the opposite of many of these statements may seem true. How were Chinese cities able to achieve many of the desirable economic and social objectives and eliminate most of the urban ills that plagued central cities around the world—poverty, crime, and inequality—under its socialist system? At whose expense did they achieve these goals? Are cities in China rapidly becoming the typical urban centers found elsewhere in the world?

This chapter tries to answer these questions by examining the central role the Chinese government played in the urbanization process. Through its administrative control over city planning and migration, the government exerted a major force on social stratification. This chapter also discusses the recent changes in the quality of life and new patterns of inequality in Chinese cities during the past two decades of economic reform.

THE HISTORICAL LEGACY

Before 1949, China had a long history of a sophisticated urban culture. Most large Chinese cities were rectangular, surrounded by a city wall (whose height was specified in imperial regulations), and crisscrossed by wide, straight boulevards that met at right angles. Often within these large blocks, there was a maze of smaller streets on which were interspersed shops and residences. Many occupations had guilds (even beggars sometimes had guilds) that regulated competition and vied for influence with the political authorities.

The early twentieth century saw a growth of modern light industry in major cities like Shanghai, yet often for export rather than for consumption in China; but smaller cities remained primarily commercial centers. The disruption of interprovincial trade during the warlord era of 1911–37 and the destruction in many cities during the Sino-Japanese War (1938–45) and the Civil War (1946–49) had a negative effect on both trade and the development of modern industry.

Planned Urbanization

Like everything else under the post-1949 Communist regime, urbanization and city life were planned and controlled through a hierarchical, bureaucratic system. The central government determined which administrative unit could be assigned a status of a city and whether it should be a state-level city (the equivalent of a province), a provincial-level city (below a province but above a county), or a county-level city (essentially a county but called a city). Since central government resources were allocated to provinces, cities, and counties according to their administrative levels, the central authority wanted to limit the number of high-ranking cities.

The success of China in limiting urban growth in the 1949–78 era can be seen in its distribution of cities by population size. By 1993, China had 570 cities, of which 10 had more than 2 million people. Forty-eight more cities had populations of at least a half-million, of which 22 were over a million people in size (State Statistical Bureau 1995b: 14). About two-thirds (342) of the cities of under a half-million had populations of less than 200,000, and 160 had populations between 200,000 and 500,000. Compared to many developing countries, China had a relatively small urban population, but it was at a higher level of industrialization. Among the urban population, there was a smaller concentration of people in a few large cities—sometimes called *primate cities*—in China than in such countries as Indonesia, Brazil, Mexico, or Korea.

Throughout the 1949–78 era, the central government tightly controlled migration to try to achieve high-speed industrialization without overheated urbanization. To maintain political and social stability and to avoid overburdening the infrastructure of the new industrial cities, the Chinese government developed an elaborate and effective household registration system, called *hu kou*, which allowed it to bring the entire population under tight control and surveillance.

Social Control

Every citizen was assigned a residence in a particular urban district or rural township, often for a lifetime. Migration without government permission was forbidden, and local police were authorized to enter a resident's home to check for and deport illegal residents. To visit relatives or friends in a different city, people from out of town were required to report to the local police station and apply for a temporary living permit. Limited relocation was sometimes possible, such as a new wife transferring to her husband's place of residence, or could be mandatory, such as a job change deemed necessary by the official labor bureau. Although the *hu kou* system had been used in prior dynasties for political control, it had never before been linked to a massive police system or used as a tool to prevent rural-urban migration.

There were also waves of reverse urbanization, when portions of the massive urban population were sent to rural areas because of urban economic difficulties, employment pressures in the cities, or national defense goals. During the Cultural Revolution whole schools and universities were "sent down" to smaller towns and cities, and toward the end of this social movement (about 1969) huge numbers of urban youths (for whom no urban jobs existed) were sent down (*xia-xiang,* pronounced shah-shiang) to rural villages. They found the standards of living in villages far below what they were used to, and many of these sent-down youth spent much of the 1970s trying to get permission to return to their urban homes.

The Communist regime was also adept at organizing city life in such a way as to reduce the possibility that deviance could pass undetected. "Cities are subdivided into districts, wards, and finally into small units of some 15 to 30 households, such as all those in one apartment building or on a small lane" (DeGlopper 1988: 135). Housewives, retired people, or others who were often home were formed into neighborhood committees, which were supposed to put up propaganda, address neighborhood problems, and detect crime and deviance.

Social Stratification

To the rural population, the household registration system was a brutal denial of their pursuit of urban job opportunities and a better quality of life. This, arguably, resulted in a much greater degree of rural-urban inequality than in many Third World countries, where rural migrant workers routinely ended up in central city slums. Within cities, the patterns of stratification and inequality in prereform China (before 1978) were determined by economic segmentation.

Workers in China are stratified along workplace ownership hierarchies. Workers in large firms or factories in the state sector usually share the same housing unit and enjoy the best economic benefits (wages, housing, medical care, pensions) and social prestige. These privileged work units (*danwei*) provided literally cradle-to-grave benefits for their workers. They are followed by workers in small state firms, workers in the urban collective sector (the nonstate municipal or neighborhood industries), and workers in the rural collective sector. Last in reward and prestige come workers in the agricultural sector, that is, farmers (Lin and Bian 1991; Walder 1992; Bian 1994). These patterns of socialist inequality were rooted in the central system of resource allocation, which fully controlled the limited opportunities for social mobility. Certain groups, such as urban residents or children of state sector workers, were systematically favored in getting access to the opportunities for getting ahead (Szelényi 1983: 43–64; Lin and Bian 1991; Walder 1992; Bian 1994).

Urban Inequality under Socialism

Socialist governments routinely claimed that the superiority of socialism over capitalism lies not only in its high rate of economic growth but also in its ability to achieve economic and social equality and dignity among all citizens. However, consistent empirical findings suggest that they have failed to reach either goal. There are two major patterns of inequality that can be identified in most socialist societies.

The first pattern is sector differentiation, both along rural-urban dimension and between different industrial sectors. Socialist industrialization usually transferred the agricultural surplus to the industrial sectors. When rural-urban migration was forbidden and transportation was primitive, it was very difficult for farmers to reach the higher-quality education and medical care provided by the state in central cities. At the same time as urban-rural sector differentiation and inequality were created in East Europe (Szelényi, 1983) and China (Lin and Bian 1991), the industrial labor force became segmented, ranging from technocrats and skilled workers in large state enterprises to unskilled seasonal laborers and the self-employed. Those engaged in heavy industry were considered contributing the most to the economy and were rewarded accordingly in terms of promotion opportunities, income, housing, and social mobility for their children. As a result, Chinese peasants aspired to become workers, and workers in peripheral sectors struggled to move up into the core sector, simply because of the systematic and unequal distribution of opportunities.

The second pattern of inequality was mainly a result of competition for bureaucratic entitlement to privileges. Scholars and journalists who failed to see inequality in socialist societies had measured inequality in terms of income and ownership of property, yet what was most unequally allocated and distributed in these societies were the access to quality goods and services and the opportunity for upward mobility. If the position as a Chinese factory manager provides an individual with excellent housing, free medical care, excellent schools for his or her child, frequent invitations to work-unit funded banquets, and a limousine and driver, the supposedly low salary goes a lot further than that of the ordinary worker.

The socialist states not only claimed that their ideological goal was to distribute resources and rewards equally, they also believed that they had done so, because they had successfully eliminated the key source of inequality and exploitation for Marxists—private ownership of the means of production. Their efforts to promote the goal of equality were focused on a relentless campaign to eradicate private ownership and market mechanisms for distributing goods and services. Ironically, by doing so, they created and intensified exactly what they were trying to get rid of—inequality.

While reform seems to be widening the urban income strata of these previously planned economies, the effect of the market is still largely to provide some correction, namely, to balance the negative effect of administrative mechanisms on social equality. Many of those in small or private enterprises, who were poorly rewarded through administrative means, are getting rich very rapidly by responding to market needs. People who were rewarded well during the administrative coordination and the extensive industrialization period—party bureaucrats and skilled workers in heavy industry—are not finding their niche as fast as the entrepreneurs in the new situation.

Group Consumption

Shortage of Consumer Goods

The socialist economic priorities of production over consumption, heavy over light industries, and autarky (complete self-sufficiency) over trade led to chronic shortages of basic and luxury consumer goods. The public had to sacrifice the desired level of consumption, postponing or neglecting certain necessities (Kornai 1992: 170–75).

To deal with shortages of virtually all types of consumer products in the 1950s, the Chinese government launched a rationing system—a coupon was needed to buy almost everything. It was a crime to buy or sell coupons. Each urban resident was entitled to buy a ration of rice, wheat flour, and corn flour each month using grain coupons. Grocery coupons were needed to buy pork, and proof of minority status was necessary to buy beef or lamb (these meats were provided for Muslims, classified as a minority group in China). Poultry and seafood were only available during holiday seasons. Eggs, edible oil, sesame jam, and other kinds of groceries were rationed as well. Cloth coupons were needed to buy cloth or clothes.

Coupons were also needed for consumer durables such as bicycles, watches, sewing machines, TVs, and refrigerators. These coupons were under the control of directors of work units, who could distribute them at their own discretion. Since these products were not considered necessities of life but were in even greater demand, both for use and as status symbols, favoritism and corruption were inevitable in distributing the coupons within a work unit. During the 1980s, rationing and coupons for consumer goods in China gradually disappeared as more goods became available through the private market. For high-demand goods, price rather than coupons became the way of determining who got what.

Remaining Legacies

Recent evidence from the former Soviet Union shows that the elimination of central bureaucratic coordination did not truly empower the workers, nor has it reversed the patterns of socialist inequality (Connor 1991; Burawoy and Krotov 1992). Few opportunities were opened up for the workers (Milor 1994). Polarized by the reform agenda as well as fearful of loss of security, workers developed a strong rank-and-file conservatism and passivity toward reforms; they distrusted glasnost and perestroika as being elitist and of benefit only to the intelligentsia (Connor 1991: 263–67, 293). Since relatively few state enterprise workers have actually lost their jobs in China as a consequence of economic reform, it is difficult to predict what the reaction of this once politically powerful group will be as China moves to the painful stage of economic restructuring, which the government claims it will do in the next several years.

THE CHANGING URBAN LANDSCAPE DURING ECONOMIC REFORMS

Urban economic reforms started in Chinese cities in the early 1980s and were aimed at improving productivity and raising the standard of living. They have generated both positive and negative results. While the urban nonstate sector economy experienced enormous growth, many money-losing state enterprises continued to fail to compete in the marketplace. The overall quality of life has been improved as a result of increased income and an abundant supply of consumer goods. Yet some workers from failed state enterprises have had a hard time finding alternative means of making a living. As the market economy stimulated entrepreneurial activities, economic and social inequality has widened. Although much more rural-urban migration is now possible, urban society has become more stratified.

Migrant Workers: Fourth-Class Citizens

The most visible change that came to large cities in the 1980s in China, other than the newly constructed high-rise buildings, was the waves of migrant workers taking over all sorts of urban jobs. Although the household registration system was kept in place, the ban on migration was less rigorously enforced after the early 1980s. The breakthrough began in the menial work that most city dwellers loathed. The need for housemaids first brought millions of rural female youth to the cities and into urban families. Soon, accelerated infrastructural development absorbed rural laborers into construction work, especially the building of roads, high-rise buildings, and airports.

Gradually, more and more migrants were hired into state and joint-venture factories, hotels, restaurants, and so on as contract workers. Urban enterprises, which were under increasing market competition, found that one way to improve productivity was to replace urban work-ers with rural workers, who demanded lower wages and few benefits and were more motivated to work. Although contract labor by rural workers had been a feature of Chinese industry before 1978 (Walder 1986: 48–54), managers were now driven to find rural workers more by the profit motive than by seeking to fulfill output quotas demanded by annual or five-year plans.

Later on, rural entrepreneurs invaded the cities by opening restaurants, hair salons, convenience stores, and various repair shops. Before 1978, Chinese cities were remarkable for the limited number of services that were available: It was often hard to get a meal outside of a factory canteen, especially at odd hours, or to get shoes repaired or buy an umbrella in one's own neighborhood. Rural dwellers began to fill these niches, first by strolling around offering goods and services, then by staying in an urban outdoor market, and finally by renting a store-front. More successful entrepreneurs included the contractors who ne-gotiated large city projects, wholesalers who provided groceries for many city stores, and factory owners who manufactured products for urban residents.

As more rural migrants gathered in a city, regional or ethnic com-munities emerged. In Beijing, for example, there are Zhejiang Village, Anhui Village, and Xinjiang Village on the city's outskirts. These com-munities are based on shared ethnic or regional origin (in this case, mi-grants from these three provinces, all of whom speak distinctive dialects) and are governed by community leaders. Zhejiang Village had many small repair shops and tailors, Anhui Village was a good place to find a maid or nanny, and Xinjiang Village was home to Uighur minority, who often found employment as butchers and itinerant shish kebab sellers. Since they were not administratively affiliated with the host city, they enjoyed a high degree of autonomy.

Because these migrants frequently encountered hostility from other urban residents, whether from natives or other rural migrants, and be-cause they lacked political, economic, and social support, the communal solidarity of these villages tends to be high. Their settlements resemble the ethnic enclaves in U.S. cities where new immigrants first settled. The Chicago university office of one of the authors stands on the site of an early twentieth-century winter Gypsy encampment bordered by Greek-town and an Italian neighborhood, all made up of separate groups of Eu-ropean migrants who bonded together for the same reasons as the provincial migrants in Beijing almost a century later.

Many urban residents or suburban farmers sell fruits, vegetables, and meat on tables set up along city streets.

Although rural migrants made significant contributions to the economic vitality of cities, they had the lowest social status in the cities and urban dwellers felt ambivalent about their presence. At a five-star hotel in Beijing, a receptionist from rural Anhui province found that hotel employees were divided into four classes, not based on their qualifications or positions but on their personal backgrounds. The first-class citizens were foreigners, including Chinese from Hong Kong or Taiwan. The second-class citizens were Beijing residents. The third-class citizens were migrant workers from nearby villages. The fourth-class citizens were migrant workers from other provinces. The receptionist had a high school diploma and was capable at her work, but she was still treated as a fourth-class citizen even though many of her fellow workers from Beijing had less education and were not at her level of efficiency.

City dwellers frequently complained about the rural migrants for their contribution to inconvenience and crime. The overcrowding on city buses and subways was associated with migrant workers, their family members, and their oversized luggage. The increased rate of theft (pickpockets are now common on crowded city buses) and other crimes were also associated in the public mind with an increased migrant population. As a result, many cities began to issue temporary residence cards to noncity residents. A card would not be issued or could be revoked if the applicant had a criminal record or if there was no proof of employment.

The huge waves of migration to Chinese cities are strikingly seasonal: During the winter slack season, rural migrants take trains or buses
to major cities to try their luck at finding work. They are often described,
almost fearfully, in the Chinese press as *mangliu* (pronounced mahng-
leo), or "blind currents" of migration:

> Waiting for employment in the morning, a large number of migrant work-
> ers squatted in the [railway] stations' hallways and front yards. Many oth-
> ers spilled over to the nearby market streets and public parks. Mostly in
> their 20s and 30s, they were almost uniformly identifiable by their shoulder-
> bags, which carried the travel documents, some simple tools, and a few
> clothes. (Hsieh 1993: 89)

As Hsieh points out, these rural migrants do not come simply for economic reasons but also because of the vague hope of obtaining urban residence or simply for the experience of visiting a big city: "One young
man made this earnest statement: 'After the city experiences, I am not a
country-bumpkin any more. I shall have a better chance to secure a bride
in my village'" (p. 91). In some ways, the most frightening thing about
these rural migrants to urban dwellers may be that it reminds them of
the huge gulf between their life chances and those of the majority of Chinese who must live in the countryside.

From a Shortage Economy
to a Mixed Economy

For most city dwellers, the quality of life has improved significantly over
the last two decades. Market reforms stimulated both agricultural and
industrial growth, and shortages of consumer goods have eased. The
early rationing system was no longer necessary and was abandoned. In
addition, the quality of consumer goods and services began to improve.
Communist political leaders usually saw the production of consumer
goods as simply taking needed resources away from producer goods or
military needs; hence there was little attention to quality. If there is a
shortage of bicycles, even the most poorly made ones will eventually be
purchased. The competition that state industries began to receive from
nonstate producers meant that they no longer had a monopoly on the
market; they had to begin to think about questions of reliability, consumer taste, and style.

Rapid economic growth, however, did induce pressures toward
inflation, and price increases (often running at 25 percent per year or
more in the late 1980s) became a major concern of most city residents.
Since employees of state industries received few raises relative to
those in the market-oriented sectors of the economy, their wages
began to decline, as did their social and economic status. The **iron rice
bowl** (*tie fan wan*, pronounced tyeh-fahn-wahn), or permanent job security, began to look far less attractive as state wages failed to keep up
with inflation.

Differentiation of Urban Social Groups

In addition to bringing rural migrants into cities, economic reforms changed previous views of social status. State sector workers and intellectuals were among the losers. The status of state sector workers declined dramatically. Compared with workers at foreign or joint-venture (mixed foreign-Chinese ownership) enterprises, the wages of state sector workers were the lowest. They also had less job autonomy and fewer opportunities for career advancement.

At the same time, scientists, engineers, school teachers, and college professors, whose income largely depended on government support, did not gain much benefit from the market transition process. Once highly regarded for both prestigious work and stable income, intellectual positions were no longer considered desirable. One common saying (a pun in Chinese) was that the fellow who sold boiled tea-eggs on the street made more money than the rocket scientist in the new economy.

Among the winners in the new system, entrepreneurs had the highest income and gradually gained wider social recognition and respect. At the beginning of the reform period, this term was associated with people with criminal records and others who were not qualified for public sector jobs (see Chapter 10). There was also strong suspicion that they made money through illegal or unethical means. Recently, however, many entrepreneurs have become inspiring role models and enjoyed favorable publicity.

These entrepreneurs formed the new rich strata in China; many of them routinely engaged in conspicuous consumption. Some of the entrepreneurs were talked about as "big boss accompanied by a young mistress." These *dakuan* (pronounced dah-kwan), or "fat cats," are now just as well-known as their Singapore, Taiwan, or Hong Kong opposite numbers for their financial acumen and free-spending ways (Kristof and WuDunn 1994: 215). In the period before the 1980s, restaurants might be full of state enterprise managers or officials holding business lunches or dinners at their work units' expense. Now, many of the most expensive restaurants and hotels in major cities are no longer oriented toward foreign tourists; instead, they count these *dakuan* as their most important customers. Exclusive private social clubs with initiation fees of U.S. $10,000 to $20,000 have emerged in Beijing, and they are already oversubscribed. Price is no object; conspicuous consumption is.

A CHANGING URBAN CULTURE

The Change in Housing

Most city residents live in state-subsidized housing, but many of the spare, poorly built 1950s and 1960s apartment buildings have been torn down because they stood on very valuable central-city land. They have been replaced by better-quality high-rise apartment buildings. The majority of these new apartments were built by work units for their employees, but more and more are built by private developers for sale to entrepreneurs, Overseas Chinese investors, or high government officials. In fact, the new and old housing built by state enterprises for their workers are seen as financial millstones around the necks of these units. To compensate for low wages, low rents are charged to state employees; however, often these hardly pay for maintenance or repairs, much less paying the enterprise back for their construction. One significant advantage joint-venture firms or township and village enterprises (TVEs) have over state enterprises is that they do not have to expend scarce capital on housing (*Far Eastern Economic Review* October 23, 1997: 85).

The state has announced plans to stop the future allocation of state-subsidized housing in late 1998, to increase the availability of mortgages for private buyers, and to "allow people to buy and sell their homes freely for the first time in five decades" (*The Wall Street Journal* March 27, 1998). A number of localities are trying to develop schemes to move urban workers into the housing market; one of the most ambitious, run by the Shanghai municipality, requires a contribution of 6 percent of monthly salary by both workers and enterprises to fund construction of new apartments and low-interest mortgage loans (a new concept in China) that will be made available to workers (*Far Eastern Economic Review* October 23, 1997: 86).

Consumer Durables

Most apartments now have a telephone; while many apartments do not come with hot water, tenants often install a natural gas or electric water heater. A 1997 book estimated that among urban households, 87 percent have a small washing machine (few have dryers), 89 percent have a refrigerator, 90 percent have a color television, and more than a quarter have a video camera or air conditioner (*Far Eastern Economic Review* November 27, 1997: 7). Many urban Chinese are running into the "Japanese problem" of lots of money to buy electronic devices but less and less room to store them in cramped living quarters.

In recent years, it has become fashionable to spend money on furniture; some residents engage in major renovation projects, including the replacement of hardwood floors, window treatments, and even enlisting the advice of interior decorators. Automobile ownership is becoming more common in urban China, especially in smaller cities, where it is easier to find parking.

The Western Influence

Japanese electronic products first invaded China in the late 1970s. Soon, the Chrysler Cherokee became Beijing Jeep through a joint venture. Greater Western influence came when chain restaurants like Kentucky Fried Chicken (a particular favorite in China), McDonald's, Pizza Hut, and Subway opened their operations on city streets and in train stations, and their advertising became ubiquitous as well. Foreign products and a foreign lifestyle were pursued as symbols of class and modernity, even if there were local adaptations: Local youth in the 1980s, for example, would often wear sunglasses with the price tag still on so that their friends would know that they were foreign ones.

Urban China today is a surprisingly cosmopolitan place. City youth dote on Italian shoes, Gucci accessories, and Japanese cosmetics. The National Basketball Association playoffs are broadcast live (in Chinese translation) and are very popular; all the major stars, such as Patrick Ewing, Shaquille O'Neill, Scottie Pippen, and of course Michael Jordan (*qiao-dan*, pronounced chow-dahn) have Chinese names. Professional soccer from Europe is also very popular, and urban males are often familiar with the players and their styles of play. In fact, if one was to measure the internationalism of big-city Chinese, they would probably rank high compared to residents of similar cities in other nations.

Emerging Social Problems

Various social problems reemerged or were aggravated during rapid social and economic changes in Chinese cities. Crime, drug addiction, prostitution, and other forms of deviant behavior were all on the rise in recent years. Traveling by train during the Cultural Revolution, one was often overwhelmed by the slogans on the sign posts along the tracks like "Long Live Chairman Mao!" "Socialism Is the Best System!" or "To Hell with Imperialism!" Traveling by train during the 1970s or 1980s, one was reminded of the "One Couple, One Child" policy. Taking a train nowadays one might see, in addition to the waves of commercial advertisements, slogans like "One Husband One Wife, Forbid Polygamy!"

Tensions in the System

Though economic growth may eventually make everyone better off, the income gap between a relatively few rich entrepreneurs and the vast majority of low-income urban residents who are paying the price of market transition can stir up strong public sentiments. These increases in income differentials will have a tremendous social impact because they are also happening at a time when what used to be free entitlements are having expensive price tags attached, such as housing, education, medical care, and other welfare facilities. According to recent survey data on public opinions in changing socialist societies, dissatisfactions usually center on the following issues.

The first has to do with the public image of societal wealth as zero-sum, or the theory of the limited good (if you're getting more, the rest of us must be getting less), and the public view of the emerging class of small and private entrepreneurs, the *getihu* (pronounced geh-tee-who). While the majority of socialist citizens understand that the past artificial egalitarian system was not true equality, many find it hard to believe that they can get rich through legal means without hurting others and deserve the reward. Data on public opinion of East European citizens also showed strong passivity and cynicism to reform. Many respondents did not approve of what was happening, nor did they indicate clear and stable political and economic preferences, and yet they did not want to emigrate to a different country.

The second widely shared concern is about uncontrolled official corruption and illegal profiteering. The decentralization of authority and a money-oriented mentality may lead party bureaucrats and government officials at various levels to use their positions and authority for personal economic gains. This, as much as vague notions of democracy, was one of the direct causes of the 1989 Tiananmen student demonstration in Beijing, as well as for the widespread popularity of their cause. Income inequality and unequal opportunities of mobility of this kind can easily delegitimate the government's efforts for political and economic reforms (Oi 1992). One of China's greatest long-run problems is that business must be conducted through a web of personal connections (*guanxi;* see Chapter 3) and without any enforceable system of contracts or business law. Since almost all business in China requires interaction with government officials, such *guanxi* networks afford ample opportunity for graft and corruption to get things done, or at least to get them done quickly.

Third, the negative effects of reform on equality are often borne, temporarily at least, by economically and socially vulnerable groups: the retired, the disabled, and the nonworking poor (Szelényi, 1989). For example, when asked which of the 18,000 miners he plans to fire over the next three years at a coal mine with 34,000 workers in poverty-stricken Ningxia , the mine manager replied bluntly: "The sick, the elderly, and the handicapped" (*The Wall Street Journal* June 1, 1998: A-1). Some speculate the current generation of urban elderly may be the last to enjoy relatively generous retirement benefits. China has its own version of the U.S. baby boomer/Social Security problem, which is compounded by the virtual bankruptcy of a large proportion of state enterprises that cannot even pay current workers much less fund future retirees (*Far Eastern Economic Review* October 23, 1997: 82).

SUMMARY

Urban life was organized to conform to the Communist ideology that emphasized growth over consumption, equality over efficiency, and group identity over individualism. First, industrial growth was achieved through bureaucratic control over production and consumption with minimal and highly restricted urbanization, which led to a persistent pattern of social immobility and inequality. Second, to achieve a high rate of growth, the state maintained the quality of urban life at a subsistence level for years. Third, deepening market reforms gradually brought China onto a capitalist track, gaining both economic prosperity and increased social inequality.

Chinese urban dwellers now find their cities strikingly different places from two decades ago. Life is much more uncertain, in both positive and negative senses, on a number of dimensions, including job and marital stability, crime, and opportunities for mobility. A 1990 survey by social scientists in Shanghai found that among the municipality's 13.5 million residents, an estimated 200,000 had severe mental disorders and another 400,000 to 500,000 had less severe ones (*Far Eastern Economic Review* April 10, 1997: 43). Anxiety, stress, and depression, while always present in China, seem to have increased in the highly competitive, pressure-filled centers of rapid economic development.

CHAPTER 9

Rural Industrialization and Recent Social Change

There are districts in which the position of the rural population is that of a man standing permanently up to the neck in water, so that even a ripple is sufficient to drown him.

R.H. Tawney 1932: 77

Scholars describing rural life in prerevolutionary China found it easy to catalog the conditions that left much of the population so close to a subsistence existence that, as Tawney points out, a good number perished every year. Chinese farmers faced a lack of land, high rents, insecure land tenancy, costly credit, and rapacious local governments that sometimes collected taxes for years in advance. In many ways, pre-1949 China seemed to be in a classic Malthusian situation, where population growth had so outstripped the productive capacity of the land that most of the population was impoverished. Although the 1949 revolution solved some of these problems, scholars writing in the 1950s (Ho 1959) predicted that further rural population growth in many provinces was unlikely, since the land could not support more people.

Yet between 1953 and the early 1990s, China's population doubled, from about 580 million to 1.2 billion, and most of that increase in population was in rural areas. (Due to changing definitions of urban and rural over the decades, it is hard to specify exactly what proportion was absorbed where.) There was terrible suffering in the Chinese countryside during the 1959–61 era, when about 30 million, largely unnecessary, deaths occurred (see Chapter 2); but even this was only a slight deviation in the trend toward increasing population density. In much of China, the need was to find jobs and subsistence for more and more rural people.

In China, only about one acre in ten is suitable for farming, whereas in the United States, about 20 percent of the nation's total area can be used for crops. Because of the lack of available farmland, almost all of the land has already been used, and the ratio of farmers to farmland in China is very high. By the mid 1980s, the Chinese rural labor force was about 370 million people, distributed across 358 million acres of cultivated cropland.

Thus the average Chinese farmer only had about 0.97 acres of farmland to cultivate. In the United States in 1992, about 295.9 million acres of land were planted, out of 945.5 million acres of farmland (U.S. Census Bureau 1996: 661). There were about 2.1 million workers with farming occupations in the United States in 1990 (Anderton et al. 1997: 606); hence there were about 140.9 acres of cultivated cropland per person in the agricultural labor force in the United States in the early 1990s.

Chinese agriculture is also handicapped by the small average size of farm. In the United States in 1992, almost 80 percent of all cultivated cropland was in farms of 500 acres or more, and over half was in farms of 2,000 acres or more (U.S. Census Bureau 1996: 661). Farms of this size in China are only possible in a few areas, such as in the Northeast, and the cost of the necessary inputs of farm machinery to cultivate such a large tract make such farming methods out of reach for almost all farm families. This ecological constraint of land scarcity in China's rural areas has existed for perhaps two centuries or more, and it has been slowly getting worse. What makes China unique among modern nations is the wide variety of solutions that have been proposed, and at least partially implemented, to let the agricultural population escape from the Malthusian trap of a near-subsistence daily existence. To understand the present rural policies we must look into the recent past.

THE DISTINCTIVENESS OF RURAL CHINA

On the surface, it seems that Chinese cities, with their rapid economic growth, large migrant populations, increased income disparity, increased Western cultural penetration, and rising crime rates, are looking more and more similar to large cities in many other Third World countries. Yet rural Chinese society, even though undergoing a rapid social and economic transformation, has continued to be distinctively Chinese. This distinctiveness lies mainly in the adherence to tradition, but another factor has been the unique path taken by Chinese peasants to pursue prosperity and modernization since 1949.

The unique features of rural development in modern China include limited out-migration to the cities, rural industrialization based on indigenous technology, agricultural de-collectivization and re-collectivization during the reform period, local government officials as corporate leaders or business brokers, new kinds of entrepreneurship, and widening rural social and economic inequality.

Legacies of the Bamboo Wall

What has made China different from many other developing countries is that, from the late 1950s till the late 1970s, migration was strictly prohibited through a nationwide, tightly administered household registration system. Jobs were not available to nonlocal residents, and any extended stay without a valid local household registration card could invite severe punishment. Through this system social order and full employment in the cities were maintained, and farmers were deprived of the right and opportunity to urban living and industrial jobs. The government has only recently given up its strict rules prohibiting human migration. The legacy of this prohibition has remained after the official ban on migration. Because employment in the urban state sector is actually decreasing, new job opportunities there are generally not sufficient to solve the urban unemployment problem, much less provide jobs for rural migrants.

What made China different from other socialist countries in the 1950s through late 1970s and early 1980s was that China has had an increasing surplus of labor that could not be absorbed by industrialization in the urban state sector. China's post-1950 baby boom, a much higher rate of infant and child survival after 1950 (see Chapter 2), and the recruitment of women into the rural labor force during the 1950s all led to a huge growth in the rural labor force since about 1965.

The government tried to relieve some of this pressure for rural jobs by encouraging the growth of local rural industry from the late 1960s on. China has a long tradition of rural industry (such as silk, handicraft, and pottery production) in many areas, and the decentralization of industry was also seen as a means of defense from foreign attack. However, other policies, such as relocating perhaps 10 million unemployed urban young people (sent-down youth) in the countryside during the 1969–76 period only exacerbated the rural employment problem.

Paradoxically, preventing those with the best education and most talent from migrating to urban areas may have forced them to tie their own success in life to local industrial and farming ventures. Byrd and Lin have pointed out that the "stable membership" of China's rural communities enabled them to retain cohesion and human resources (Byrd and Lin 1990: 4), which is often a key problem in communities undergoing rapid social change. In addition, while not all sent-down youth were welcomed in villages in the early 1970s because they represented extra mouths to feed, they had far more education than most villagers and brought with them a knowledge of the outside world.

Agricultural Collectivization

Since 1949, the Chinese rural society has undergone and is still undergoing fundamental changes. Land reform, which started nationwide in 1950 as the Communists took control of the country, redistributed the land of the rural elite to the rural masses. Soon after that, the government launched a rural collectivization campaign; and agricultural production and rural life were organized into different levels of collectives by 1956.

Collective agricultural production existed for more than two decades in rural China and served both ideological and economic purposes. From the point of view of Communist ideology, getting rid of the landowning classes and organizing peasants into collective units decreased the power of class enemies and raised the revolutionary consciousness of the peasantry. From an economic point of view, the Chinese government found it far easier to deal with large collective farms to make sure that needed grain was delivered to the state in accordance with the state plan.

Chinese rural society under Maoist rule pursued four basic strategies of economic and social development: collective organization of all farm work, diversification of rural economic activities, gradual extension of basic health and education programs, and creation of a local administrative structure of commune-brigade-production team with varying degrees of autonomy and control over surpluses (Aziz 1978).

From the late 1950s until 1978, almost all Chinese farmers were organized in work units of about 20–40 households called production teams. These production teams were organized into production brigades comprised of about 100 to 350 households; the production teams tended to "encompass a single large village or several small villages" (Parish and Whyte 1978: 36). Decisions about production would be made at the team or brigade level, and the income (in cash or the crop itself) of the team or brigade would be shared among its members. In most cases, farmers would receive work points for the tasks they accomplished, and the annual total of these work points could then be exchanged for an appropriate share of the team's or brigade's income. Only during a few periods, such as the "free supply" era during the Great Leap Forward in 1958, were farm households given their income on the basis of need rather than for labor contributed.

The strengths and weaknesses of collective farming are apparent. According to Perkins (1988), the collective approach led to China's success in rural economic development because the government was (1) capable of mobilizing the entire rural population for economic production through bureaucratic and party channels and (2) committed to letting the peasants have a large share of benefits of programs being implemented in the countryside.

On the other hand, the excessive use of bureaucratic forms of resource allocation in agriculture, rather than market forces, in the 1960s and 1970s created economic inefficiencies that offset the gains resulting from the use of scientific farming and modern technology. Also, the suppression of the market and abandoning comparative advantage and interregional trade for self-sufficiency resulted in persistent poverty in some parts of the country. Rabushka (1987) and others suggest that lack of market incentives explain why Maoist China was unable to grow as rapidly as Taiwan or Hong Kong did during the same period.

De-Collectivization

Starting in 1979, rural China adopted a mode of production with the individual household as the unit of production. This process of dismantling joint work and accounting units is called *de-collectivization,* and it greatly raised farmers' initiative and boosted agricultural production.

The state granted a long-term lease to each farming household, which was responsible for the cultivation and maintenance of its land. After meeting the state's quota obligation, by either turning in part of the crop or by paying cash, the household was free to keep any surplus from the land. Farm workers were no longer paid for their labor through work points, which previously had allowed them a share of the collective's output. Instead, individual households made decisions about how labor was to be allocated. Farm animals and equipment that previously belonged to the collectives were also assigned to the households. By 1983, 95 percent of the rural areas in China had adopted the **household responsibility system** (Parish 1985: 18).

This new system of production increased incentives and improved the efficiency of farming. Farmers usually were far more willing to work harder when they knew they would get to keep the profits and eager to improve the soil on land they knew they would be cultivating in later years. An initial rapid increase in agricultural production was achieved through farmers' responses to market needs, by cutting costs at the household level, by diversifying agricultural activities according to local climate, land, and other conditions, and by accelerating the process of combining traditional practices with modern technology (Wittwer 1987). Many local adaptations of policy were made; in some cases, such as in terms of collective ownership of agricultural machinery, it made economic sense to retain some elements of the old system along with the new (Zweig, 1989).

Re-Collectivization

As market reforms penetrated Chinese rural society during the late 1980s and early 1990s, and the number of rural unemployed and underemployed grew, more and more farmers migrated to find jobs in the cities or in local industrial enterprises. Many of them simply returned their unused farmland to the village, which had to manage the land collectively using women who remained in the village and migrant laborers from other areas. Because of these trends, some Western scholars have warned that China might follow trends in Japan and Korea and experience a shortage of agricultural labor and thus a decline in agricultural output. A potential food shortage for a country with 1.2 billion people could be devastating not only for China but also to the entire world.

In rural areas around central cities and along the southeastern coast, there has been a rapid outflow of farmers to work as temporary laborers in the cities or to work at local industrial enterprises. In fact, rural industries in some areas expanded so fast that outside workers were recruited, often from distant provinces. Between 1978 and 1988, employment at such nonfarm rural enterprises rose from 28.3 to 95.4 million people

(Yang 1996: 214). Yet the scenario of a shortage of agricultural labor supply seems far-fetched, at least considering the size of the overall rural population in China and the uneven development of rural industrialization throughout the country.

Recent migration in China exhibits two patterns: from the countryside to the urban areas, and from the western inland provinces to coastal areas. In both cases, more and more farmers from remote places have started working on the land in suburban and coastal villages where the locals have found nonfarm jobs. For the migrant farmers, the incentive was to receive higher economic returns from farming and the possibility to eventually move up to a nonfarm position.

The challenge here was to re-collect the vacant land previously allocated to each household and organize the migrant farmers coming from various parts of the country to work together. This job often fell to village heads, who had the management skills and economic incentives to do it. Since in many areas (especially in prosperous, better-educated ones) village head is now an elective position, these leaders now have added incentive to organize farm production in a way that satisfies their constituents. In a way, re-collectivization was different from collectivization in the 1950s because it was voluntary and economic rather than compulsory and ideological. It was similar to Western-style commercialization of farming in that it was designed to achieve economies of scale and to put unused resources (land) to good use.

Rural Economic Vitality

Rural industry emerged in China soon after the land reform, but its growth did not accelerate until the early 1970s. Political, social, and economic conditions contributed to the development of rural industry in China. This nation is a combination of diverse phenomena: a powerful authoritarian central government whose legitimacy is increasingly challenged by the citizens at large; an alienated population fed up with government corruption, inflation, and increasing social inequality; and yet a soaring national economy and rapid growth of personal wealth, which, of course, was starting from a very low level in 1979.

Much of China's economic success has been in the nonstate, mostly rural sector where the political center has the least control and local governments the most. The linkage of rural local enterprises, whether backed by local public or private money (the line here is often indistinct), to world markets has provided China with a means of both soaking up the rural unemployed and generating needed foreign exchange.

The nonstate sector is simply any and all of the economic activities that are not centrally planned or coordinated. The largest nonstate sector is composed of the rapidly expanding collectively owned enterprises and of privately owned businesses. The economic reforms in China during the past decade and a half can be visualized as the rise of the nonstate sector and a corresponding decline of the state sector (State Statistical Bureau 1995a).

The Local Corporatist Hypothesis

Compared with other socialist or former socialist countries, China has enjoyed some unique conditions favorable to the rapid expansion of its nonstate sector economy. Historically, as many scholars have pointed out, the Chinese socialist system was less centralized due to the lack of bureaucratic capacity and has always relied on local governments' initiatives for various social, economic, and political purposes (Lindblom 1977). Coming largely from the countryside, the Chinese government leadership encouraged rural infrastructure construction and small-scale industry, utilizing inexpensive rural labor. The model of rural economy in the former Soviet Union, on the other hand, suffered severely from overcentralization, a costly emphasis on agricultural mechanization, and huge, inefficient state farms (Ellman 1989).

Moreover, a gradual political decentralization since reform has allowed the local government to gain greater control over local resources. Byrd and Lin (1990) and Oi (1992) have pointed out that the change in the power base and legitimacy of local government officials has transformed them from simply carrying out orders from above to the active promotion of rural industrialization, often on their own initiative. This "local corporatist" hypothesis suggests that the role of local cadres underwent a fundamental transformation during the reform era.

The choice of what kind of local collective industry to encourage is often pragmatic. Since farmers have largely turned to the markets, they have become less dependent on the local government. Farming is no longer a large source of revenue for local governments. Local officials still have to find employment opportunities for school-leavers or be faced with unhappy youth with no money and lots of time on their hands, a dangerous combination in any nation. Since promoting private industry might be politically risky, the local state finds rural industry as a way out of this dilemma.

The Township and Village Enterprises

All these conditions enabled the rapid growth of China's collective sector, which is ahead of the state sector in China's economic reforms. The degree of direct ownership of such township and village enterprises varies from locality to locality and is determined by the strategy adopted by the local governments.

The local government also often directly intervenes in the management of local collective enterprises through the **contract responsibility system**. Managers are charged with the burden of running the factories efficiently and profitably, but they are deprived of the power to make key decisions regarding personnel, production, and investment changes. "Factory managers who make good suggestions or happen to run the factories targeted for development or expansion may receive large bonuses, but the engine for change and development is the local government" (Oi 1992: 119).

At the same time, "control of investment and credit decisions is one of the most effective levers used by local governments to shape the course of development" (Oi 1992: 121). Local state agencies often serve as the guarantor of an enterprise to secure a bank loan, and if necessary, local officials are often able to use personal as well as professional connections to secure investment funds. The rules by which the local government allocates scarce resources under its control is no longer considered corrupt bargaining but open and formalized favoritism, not resulting from political pressure or personal connections but based on the enterprise's potential to generate revenue for the locality. Local firms are rated on the basis of past performance, and various preferential treatments are offered accordingly.

RURAL URBANIZATION

The process of urbanization after 1949 can be divided into three phases. During the first phase, from 1949 to 1957, there was rapid rural-to-urban migration. The proportion of urban population in the entire population increased from 11 percent in 1949 to 20 percent in 1960. During the second phase, from 1961 to 1977, the country experienced severe economic difficulties in urbanization. In the early 1960s, 20 million industrial employees were sent back to their original villages. During the Cultural Revolution, millions of urban youth were sent to the countryside. In the third phase, from 1978 to the present, there has been a rapid increase in rural-urban migration and the proportion of the urban population.

As a result of government restrictions and lack of market opportunities, the process of urbanization was relatively slow in China compared with many other developing countries, but it is different from urbanization in other countries. Fei Xiaotong, the most famous sociologist in China, has summarized the unique feature of the urbanization and industrialization process in China in five words, *li tu bu li xiang,* meaning "leaving the farm but not leaving the countryside." Instead of a massive rural population moving to a few big cities, farmers are able to find industrial and service sector jobs in small towns and cities nearby and develop an urban lifestyle within a larger rural setting (Parish, Zhe, and Li 1995). The obvious advantages of this type of urbanization include a less traumatic dislocation of a large population and less burden on the services that must be provided by existing cities. To some extent, this pattern of urbanization is similar to that found in Japan of the 1950s or of Taiwan of the 1965–75 era.

Although central cities are able to provide temporary job opportunities to many migrant workers, it is not easy or possible for the already overburdened central cities to permanently absorb a large amount of the rural population. The infrastructural cost to accommodate population growth would be two to three times lower in small cities and towns than in large cities. The solution is to encourage rural industrial-ization and develop small cities and towns. According to one estimate, there are 50,000 small cities and towns with a population less than 3,000. Most of them have the potential to increase their size two to three times. This type of growth may be able to accommodate 200–300 million rural residents.

One feature of rural China that cannot be overemphasized is its di-versity. In the more industrialized and commercialized Yangtze delta near Shanghai and the Zhu River Delta near Guangzhou (in Guangdong province), rural life has taken on a completely new look. Economic growth and local infrastructural development enable many families to combine the convenience of urban living and the comfort of a rural set-ting. Cinemas, theaters, dancing halls, fancy restaurants, and karaoke places (sing-along bars and restaurants) are as popular in small towns as in large cities. When available living space, levels of pollution, and crime are taken into consideration, small towns do not necessarily have a lower living standard than big cities. In China's vast, less-developed rural in-land areas, local urbanization is also taking place.

Two-Way Migration

In addition to the major migration streams of farmers moving to big cities or settling in small towns and small cities that are rapidly industrializing and urbanizing, there are two new trends in internal migration in China.

The first is that as some small booming cities along the coast accu-mulate more investment capital and become more involved in large-scale industrial or high-tech production, they have both the need and re-sources to attract technical and professional personnel from the ailing state-owned enterprises in large cities. Many of these professionals have a hard time utilizing their skills and expertise in the large state enter-prises. The salary advantage of state organizations is also disappearing.

Rural enterprises owned by townships or private entrepreneurs also try to lure various experts with attractive salary and benefits. Some work as part-time consultants; others simply relocate from the cities. If and when these urban experts' families move there (and Chinese families are well known for their ability to tolerate long absences by spouses), they will probably also demand an upgrading of educational and cul-tural institutions.

The second trend is rural-rural migration. A large number of peas-ants from inland rural areas, or from hill and mountain regions of nearby provinces, are migrating to the coastal areas looking for jobs. Some will work in rural enterprises, others will replace local farmers whose work has shifted out of agriculture.

TRENDS IN RURAL INEQUALITY
AND STRATIFICATION

Several factors contributed to the system of limited inequality and stratification in rural China during Mao's era (1949–76). First, the major gap
in inequality was between cities and countryside as a result of the lack
of migration for the two decades after the late 1950s. Peasants throughout the country shared the same destiny because of their participation in
collective farming.

Second, agricultural policy overemphasized grain production nationwide without regard to local conditions. As a result, farmers were
unable to take advantage of the possibility of growing commercial crops
well adapted to local conditions, or they were discouraged from engaging in rural industrial activities. It is now clear that handicraft industries
and small factories in China's rural areas could have developed and participated in the East Asian trade boom in the 1960s and 1970s just as well
as their Korean or Taiwanese counterparts, had the central government
allowed them to do so.

Third, the Maoist egalitarian ideology often artificially redistributed rewards with little regard to performance, thus dampening productive initiatives among farmers and resulting in shared poverty. Finally,
to reduce regional economic and income disparities, the central government systematically extracted resources and surplus production from advanced regions for the benefit of less-developed areas.

However, external and internal economic and status disparity still
existed during Mao's era. Interregional differences in natural endow-
ment and human capital, hoarding of resources by local governments,
and policy fluctuations that sometimes favored more advanced areas all
helped maintain and sometimes aggravate economic and social inequality across the nation's rural population.

Intervillage disparities also existed. After marriage, which usually
was between couples from different villages, a groom could bring his
bride to his wealthier village, but a bride had to "marry down" to her
new husband's village. Since property usually belonged to and moved
with the male line, this led to a greater concentration of wealth in some
villages (Parish and Whyte 1978: 71–72). By the mid-1980s, Chinese demographers warned that about 40 percent of all rural counties were
below the poverty line.

Intravillage inequality was more political than economic. The former landowners and their family members were not trusted and were
deprived of most of the rights that other rural residents had because of
their "bad class background." At the same time, they were convenient
targets of criticism and denunciation during political campaigns. Those
with a poor peasant background were relied upon by the Communist
Party and assigned the leadership and the activist roles to reach and mobilize the rural masses. Although it was often difficult for village leaders
or activists to openly scoop a larger share of the agricultural surplus for

themselves, they sometimes used favoritism to determine how the resources and surpluses were distributed among villagers.

The rural economic reform that started with the household responsibility system in the late 1970s increased rural stratification along two dimensions. Economic autonomy and market incentives enabled some farmers to accumulate wealth faster than others, contributing to greater income inequality. In the 1980s, even urban residents were openly envious of successful farmers who made fortunes by starting mink farms or by supplying high-priced mushrooms to foreign buyers. Rapid rural industrialization and marketization generated a variety of new nonfarm job opportunities, leading to more rural occupational differentiation.

After almost two decades of economic reform, income disparities have been drastically enlarged among the population within and among rural communities. As Lu Xueyi, a sociologist and rural expert, succinctly put it: "In modern-day China, the poorest Chinese are in the countryside. So are the richest" (personal communication 1995). Among the 800 million rural residents, about 10 percent were still living in poverty, barely having enough food to eat and too poor to send their children to school. Conditions in many of China's poorest counties are so bad—and made worse by the fraying of the social safety net in many areas—that the government has launched Project Hope, an antipoverty program aimed at improving health and education in those areas. On the other hand, many rural entrepreneurs became extremely successful and have adopted lavish lifestyles (Li 1997). According to one estimate, there were several hundred entrepreneurs with assets of over a few hundred million yuan, and most of them had rural origins (Jiang, Lu, and Dan 1995: 166).

Rural occupational differentiation has begun to accelerate since the early 1980s, a result of rapid industrialization and marketization. According to one study, in 1997, about 60 percent of all rural residents were still engaged in agriculture, forestry, fishery, animal husbandry, or other farm-related activities(Li 1997: 94). More than 15 percent had become workers for rural collective or private enterprises. More than 7 percent were private business owners, self-employed, or business partners. Around 2 percent were rural administrators or collective enterprise managers and about 1 percent were engaged in education, health, or other public service sectors.

Rural economic inequality between the eastern coastal and the western inland areas has worsened in the last two decades. The ratio of average income between the coastal and inland regions increased from less than 3 to 1 in 1978 to 4 to 1 in 1987 (Lu 1991: 430). This income difference has gotten even larger in the past decade. It is a major factor in the huge migration of labor from China's interior (especially from Sichuan province, where about 70 million rural residents live) to the rapidly industrializing southeastern provinces (Fujian and Guangdong).

At the same time, the process of occupational differentiation was faster in more advanced rural areas. In the coastal areas, there were twice as many private business owners, partners, or self-employed people as in the western inland region. The coastal areas also had more industrial workers, administrators, and managers. In the less-developed areas, a much larger proportion of the population was still engaged in agriculture.

SUMMARY

Rural China has experienced dramatic and constant changes in the past five decades. The mode of farming and the organization of rural life shifted from private households to collectives in the mid-1950s through the late 1970s. The household responsibility system, which started in the late 1970s, reallocated agricultural land, farm equipment, and resources to private hands. Yet since the late 1980s, collective farming began to reemerge (re-collectivization) when the original farmers left the land (now farmed by migrants from poorer areas) behind them.

Rapid and continued rural industrialization will provide nonfarm jobs to the rural labor force and stimulate rural urbanization by providing the necessary infrastructure and cultural facilities. In fact, one unique feature of rural China is the booming of small towns and cities that generate economic growth and provide a new lifestyle combining rural and urban elements.

Rural society became more stratified and differentiated as a result of rapid industrialization and the growth of the market economy. Yet while rural society became more stratified, this process of economic development opened up new avenues of social mobility as well. In addition to continuing their farm tasks, more rural residents began to engage in entrepreneurial activities, rural enterprise management, industrial jobs, or public administration and services. As a result, rural income greatly increased. Just as in the United States in the 1990s, increasing levels of income inequality seem to be more tolerable if the overall standard of living is rising and if there are a variety of avenues for social mobility.

China's New Entrepreneurs: Origins, Types, and Evolution

Sociologists since the time of Durkheim, Weber, and Marx have been wrestling with why China is organized so differently from Western nations and what effects this has on its societal evolution. In the mid-nineteenth to mid-twentieth century, the emphasis was on why China never developed an independent entrepreneurial class that could have led the way to capitalism and economic growth. This is sometimes referred to as the Protestant ethic analogy.

From 1950 on, sociologists tried to explain why China seemed particularly fertile soil for Marxist (also a Western import, incidentally) forms of social organization. For the first decade or so (1949–59), scholars studied what appeared to be China's successful economic development under a centralized, Stalinist-style state. As the drawbacks of the Marxist/Leninist/Maoist model became better known, the emphasis turned to explaining its economic stagnation, its policy oscillations, and its systems of control.

The last two decades in China have been one of the most important periods of economic development in recent world history (Chapter 1). One-fifth of the world's population has seen its living standards change dramatically for the better, and most of them have confidence that these changes will continue in the future. Yet most of this change was completely unpredicted by scholars of China. The Chinese government now takes credit for much of what has happened. Yet any dispassionate examination of government plans and policies over the past two decades would probably reveal that a great deal of the government's success came from the fact that it was making up these policies as it went along, especially in the industrial area, and had little idea where things were going to end up.

The key social fact of recent Chinese economic success appears to be that all over the country, especially in areas of Guangdong province in the early 1980s, individuals and groups of people decided to take an entirely new and very risky path to self-fulfillment. While it is easy for capitalistic Americans to say that Chinese in the early 1980s wanted to get rich, it should be remembered that for three decades before 1979, trying to get rich was a quick route to a labor camp. Even if many people in poverty in China during the early reform period wanted to get rich, why did only some people take the risks, and why did an even smaller number succeed? If sociology is to make important contributions to our understanding of the world, rather than just reflecting the frequently narrow interests of its American practitioners, it must take on such big—and sometimes unclear or unwieldy—questions of modern life.

This chapter, based largely on coauthor Fang Li's field research, shows how different kinds of entrepreneurs emerged at different periods of the reform and discusses some of the problems they faced (Li 1997). We will be presenting stories here because no sociologist has yet tied up the theoretical package of how and why so many kinds of entrepreneurship took place in so many parts of China. We also use this method because this is the way in which the Chinese themselves think about entrepreneurship: It usually involves tales about successful or unsuccessful individuals rather than a set of business-school principles.

ENTREPRENEURSHIP: PRIVATIZATION CHINESE-STYLE

One hot topic among people in China nowadays is so-and-so just started a new business, or so-and-so suddenly became rich (*fa le*, pronounced fah-luh). The tone of the conversation reflects both admiration and jealousy. Even today, there is profound ambivalence about the businessman or businesswoman in China, an ambivalence that has roots in the distrust of the merchant in traditional China and the active denunciation of capitalists during most of the Communist era.

Even after economic reforms began in the early 1980s, the state professed a kind of value-neutral attitude toward entrepreneurship and the revival of capitalism. Early in the economic reform, the Chinese leader Deng Xiaoping was asked how he could justify using capitalist methods to foster economic growth. His widely quoted reply was a classic technocratic one: "Does it matter if the cat is black or white, as long as it catches mice?" Deng was clearly putting China's economic development as his key goal and suggesting that the revival of capitalism was just one useful means toward that goal. This is, of course, a less than ringing endorsement of entrepreneurship; while the state can say "It is glorious to get rich" (since the state would then have a larger fortune to tax), there is no guarantee that the state's view could not change rapidly in the future. In fact, the party recognized the perils that allowing a widening gap in income distribution could bring; it was not until the mid-1980s that it endorsed the view that some people had to be allowed to get rich first before all could prosper.

Merchants as Scapegoats in Chinese History

In Confucian thought and teaching, merchants had a low status, below that of farmers. They were seen as a kind of speculator class on whom officials should keep a close eye. When China began to modernize in the late nineteenth century, officials made various attempts to keep merchants and the new industries under their control. More realistically, of course, many officials realized that merchants could generate considerable wealth and could be squeezed for extra tax payments or bribes and even forced to provide jobs or contracts for the officials' relatives.

Before 1949, China had little tradition of private enterprise; it struck most Chinese as perfectly natural that the state should be able to control entrepreneurs, just as it did other areas of society. Many late-nineteenth-century Chinese merchants were compradors, business agents for foreign firms (Spence 1990: 224). This frequently brought them under attack by Nationalists who saw them as key links in foreign attempts to dominate China. The Communist takeover of industry in the 1950s was a more extreme version of this, but there was historical precedent. During the Five-Anti Campaign of 1952 (against "bribery, tax evasion, theft of state property, cheating on government property, and stealing state economic information"; Spence 1990: 536), many entrepreneurs had to pay huge fines, and many had their businesses confiscated by the state. Thus the social environment of the early reform era (after 1978) was not one that looked particularly promising for the emergence of independent entrepreneurs, free from government interference.

SOCIAL ORIGINS OF ENTREPRENEURS

Three patterns of post-1978 entrepreneurial development can be identified according to the social origins, market locations, and the timing of those entering the postreform private sector: the *neng ren* (able person), the *dao ye* (profiteer), and the *xia hai* (go down to the sea of commerce) entrepreneurs.

The Rural *Neng Ren* (Able Person) Entrepreneur

There are two kinds of *neng ren* (pronounced nung-wren), or able persons, who turned out to be successful entrepreneurs in rural China. The first kind were farmers with education, skills, and nonfarm experience, including returned veterans, prior to market reforms. Many of them started by leasing village land to set up animal or vegetable farms or fruit orchards or by establishing small processing or craft factories. The second kind were local officials with organizational skills and political connections. Many of them leased or purchased collective firms or became contractors for urban construction sites or owners of trucking companies.

From Egg Boy to Eel King

In 1967, Huang was 11 years old, the eldest son in an impoverished rural family of seven children. His mother was seriously ill. Unable to afford to finish primary school, he started making a living as an "egg boy" (dan zai), traveling barefoot between the village and the county town to sell eggs. During the era of class struggle (1966–78), he was often captured by the police or political activists and made an example of "the capitalist tail"; his eggs and egg basket were smashed. But he learned how to make a living, and in less than a decade these experiences helped him to become the president and CEO of a $20 million private corporation in China in 1993.

Early in the economic reform period, Huang set up a duck farm, which soon grew into a major supplier of thousands of tons of duck eggs to more than six provinces across China. Not settling for the nickname of "duck general" (ya siling), he then built an eel farm when he heard that baby eels, the feed for his ducks, were a delicacy in high demand in Japan. Yet he was soon falsely accused of smuggling eels and put in jail for more than a year.

Soon after his release from jail, he continued to develop the indigenous technology of eel farming and finally succeeded. Within a few years, his business expanded to include 10 large eel farms.

After 1990, Huang began to cooperate with universities and research institutions in China to develop health products. He said that he had relied on intuition and experience in the past, but in the future, he would base decisions on scientific analysis. He also established, among other welfare programs, a public safety fund and a preschool education fund.

The Urban *Dao Ye* (Profiteer) Entrepreneur

This group originated from the urban marginal population: ex-prisoners, school dropouts, returned educated youth previously sent to the countryside (xia xiang), and chronic job seekers. Unable to get into the prestigious state sector, they had to look for opportunities in the cracks of the system during the initial period of urban reform. Some became street vendors, selling big bowls of tea, ice cream, or souvenirs. Others opened small restaurants or hair salons. Many of them, however, became dao ye (pronounced dow-yeah), a derogatory term meaning the "master of profiteering." They became dao ye initially by partaking in such activities as selling trendy clothing shipped from the south or smuggling or pirating consumer goods like foreign-brand sunglasses or jeans.

The Myth of Mu

In less than 12 years, the legendary tycoon Mu rose from being a convict under a sentence to death to the founder of a one billion yuan ($120 million) holding company.

With a capitalist family background (zibenjia chushen), Mu was denied a college education in the 1960s. In 1975, he was sentenced to death for openly criticizing the Cultural Revolution only to have his life spared when the Gang of Four and their followers were removed from power. On the second day of his release from prison, he announced that "the party saved my life, and it has no worth except for being an experimental field for economic reforms."

Mu began his business career with a 300-yuan loan (less than U.S. $50) and a 12-square-meter leased space. After much frustration and humiliation, his Zhongde Corporation began to prosper. To show his social responsibility, he declined preferential tax treatment for his company and aggressively recruited urban youth who could not be absorbed by the state sector. Like many other successful entrepreneurs, he was put into prison on false charges of bribery, profiteering, and "spiritual pollution." While in prison, he decided to apply to the Communist Party, and was more determined to continue on his entrepreneurial course.

During the economic ups and downs in the late 1980s, Mu continued building his commercial empire, which included several trading companies, factories, and department stores. He planned to accomplish more: developing tourist areas at the Three Gorges (China's massive hydroelectric project), creating an automobile city out of Chongqing, expanding Sichuan Air Lines, building the tallest skyscraper in China, opening a university, and launching satellites.

The Urban *Xia Hai* (Sea of Commerce) Entrepreneur

Xia hai (pronounced shah-high) refers to a recent wave of the urban privileged who quit their government jobs to engage in private businesses, or to "go down to the sea of commerce." Many of these well-educated urbanites started private businesses closely related to their prior job experience: high-technology, consulting, advertising, and subcontracting. Others, with political and managerial backgrounds, used their contacts to become brokers between entrepreneurs (sometimes foreign), markets, and bureaucracies, and they made profits off real estate and other deals. A private publishing agent, who had graduated from an elite university in Beijing and worked as a reporter for a prestigious government newspaper for many years, told me during an interview that he was able to make a lot of money by hooking up writers and publishers, many of whom were his personal friends (i.e., using *guanxi*; see Chapter 3).

The Story of Liu

Admittedly, few movie stars were more successful than Liu when she decided to start her own business. Why? Filial piety. On one hot summer day in 1985, she went to visit her parents and grandmother-in-law in the condominium she bought for them with a loan from friends. She found that they were ill from the hot weather. They could have bought an air conditioner, but they could not afford to pay the electric bill. She then vowed to commit herself to a career of entrepreneurship and to make enough money to let her family live comfortably.

Praised as a "rare genius" among her business peers, Liu was a dazzling success in the real estate, cosmetics, and fashion industries. Within a few years, she became one of the wealthiest people in China. Like other legendary entrepreneurs, she was not interested in the comfort and leisure money could afford, rather, she lived a busy and simple life. Like other such heroes, she never failed to support public causes and to help people in need.

EARLY RURAL AND URBAN ENTREPRENEURSHIP

When economic reform first started in China's countryside in 1978, farmers responded to the household responsibility system, which divided the land for private farming, with enormous enthusiasm, boosting rural production to record highs in the succeeding years. The immediate success of rural economic reform helped farmers accumulate savings, which allowed those with special skills (*yiji zhichang*, pronounced yee-jee-jih-chahng) such as driving, carpentry, or craftsmanship to start their own businesses. But urban reform experiments were more tentative, granting investment and tax privileges to only four southern coastal cities identified as special economic zones. Few structural changes were made until 1984.

Urban residents, entitled to free housing, health care, and other benefits, relied on the government to deal with the two causes of low productivity associated with the socialist redistributive economy. One was the iron rice bowl (*tie fan wan*), or permanent employment from which it was virtually impossible to be fired for poor performance. The other problem was "eating from the big rice bowl" (*chi da guo fan*), or the fact that for most work units, individuals' rewards were not based on their own work performance but resulted from their own and their unit's political influence (Walder 1986). Enjoying their protected status and relatively easy lifestyle, few state sector employees were motivated to risk engaging in private businesses.

The social origins of entrepreneurs varied over time in rural and urban China. During the early stage of rural reform, farmers who were successful in agricultural activities were able to save some income. With special skills such as carpentry, driving (a relatively rare skill in China), or animal husbandry, these *neng ren* like the Eel King Huang began to enter private businesses by setting up animal farms and orchards or by leasing small collective enterprises. Some, taking advantage of their organizational skills and connections in cities, became transportation and construction contractors.

Opportunities in the urban private sector looked bleak during this period, since most city residents still enjoyed the relative advantages and security of working in the state municipal sectors. Urban youth, like the *dao ye* Mu, who were unable to find state jobs were among the first to enter the private sector, selling clothes, food, and souvenirs on the street. Though most of these urban business owners made a living by providing some sort of service, such as private restaurants or hair salons, some of them, in fact, engaged in selling smuggled and pirated products and other profiteering activities, which, of course, do not show up in standard sample surveys.

The restaurant industry, especially outdoor restaurants, are a frequent venture of entry-level entrepreneurs with little capital.

Between 1984 and 1988, the private sector experienced a boom. Successful agricultural reform and relative policy stability led more rural residents into private industry. Most noticeably, rural officials, with managerial skills and political connections, began to seek their fortunes in the marketplace as farmers became increasingly independent of officials for resources. This eroded the rural officials' basis of authority and legitimacy, as well as making their jobs less desirable.

During this period, urban economic reform was formally launched, putting pressure on state sector firms to improve productivity and competitiveness. At the same time, greater market incentives lured more people away from their state sector jobs into the private sector. Holding a second job became more common for urban residents, and some well-connected salespersons and unhappy blue-collar workers decided to become full-time entrepreneurs. Relying on special skills and ties with gatekeepers in state enterprises, some established subcontracting workshops for needed products. Many, like movie star Liu, decided to *xia hai*, or ditch a secure low-paying state sector job for adventures on the sea of commerce.

A Transitional Phase, 1989–1992

Soon after the 1989 Tiananmen Square incident, entrepreneurs were targeted by government agencies as a source of economic and ideological instability. Fearful of further harassment and persecution, some entrepreneurs handed over their companies to the government, while many others declared bankruptcy. But at the same time, people changed their attitude about politics and money: talking about the first, but working for the second.

The Tiananmen Square incident shattered the general optimism among urbanites about government-led economic development and prosperity. Many of them became much less idealistic and began whole-heartedly to pursue money by various means as soon as the government loosened its control on economic activities in 1992. In addition, government salaries had not been keeping up with inflation; also, many state sector workers' consumer dreams had expanded. In some cases, one member of a family would retain a government job, thus guaranteeing the family's housing and other state sector benefits, while another family member would plunge into the uncertain world of small business.

ALTERNATIVE SOLUTIONS

Since institution-based trust is lacking and market uncertainties are high, emerging entrepreneurs in China face formidable managerial challenges. They appear to be searching for an alternative model to supplement or supplant old-style pre-1949 family management. One possible reason for this is that after almost 50 years of Communist rule and social revolution, the extended family is no longer a strong institution (see Chapter 5) or one that can be readily adapted to the needs of modern entrepreneurship.

Exchange of Liability

Many entrepreneurs have had bad experiences with incompetent family or kin members working for them as managers or workers. Yet, constrained by family or kinship responsibilities, they are unable to dismiss these attached members, who often become bad examples in the firm and threaten the entrepreneur's authority. To shed this burden, various entrepreneurs may get together and agree to exchange job offers to each other's family members or relatives. They thus fulfill their obligation to find a job for their family members or relatives, but these new bosses are able to treat other entrepreneurs' family members or relatives working in their firms as they would other employees.

Educational Credentials and Other Complementary Qualities

Among successful entrepreneurs, many had little formal education. Yet they value education highly, and they believe that knowledge of technology and expert opinions will pay off in the marketplace. Mr. F, a primary-school dropout, whose telecommunication company was ranked among the 100 largest private manufacturers in China in 1995, hired 5 Ph.D. and 12 master's degree holders working as senior managers. The general manager was a 30-year-old Ph.D. from a famous northern university. Similarly, Mr. L, owner of six private companies in the garment, carpet, trade, and computer hardware fields, replaced all of his top managers with college graduates specializing in engineering and commerce. In addition, entrepreneurs also find ways to attract people with complementary qualities. Former state factory directors are sought for their managerial and coordinating experience, and former Communist Party secretaries of state units are hired to provide political guidance and social legitimacy. Even celebrities are paid for public relations and advertising purposes.

Material Incentives

One common way to compensate for superior performance from a manager not related by blood is money. The Mr. F mentioned above gave a year-end bonus of 800,000 yuan (about U.S. $100,000) to one sales manager who outperformed others in the company. Local government bureaucrats who accompanied us during this fieldwork interview were stunned by this amount, which was hundreds of times more than their annual salaries. Entrepreneurs routinely paid their top managers extremely well in salary and benefits in order to get the best performance out of them.

Learning from State Enterprises

Perhaps due to the lack of other models to follow, entrepreneurs in China sometimes try to imitate what state enterprises do in management. Ironically, this is exactly why many state firms are not very efficient. For example, most entrepreneurs provide some form of medical insurance, housing, pension, and other benefits to their employees. At the same time, research showed that many private firms not only formed departments to manage their business activities, they also created and incorporated unions, employee assemblies, and even Communist Party branch offices inside their firms. According to the institutional theory of organization, much of this was geared to gain legitimacy rather than for efficiency.

Looking West

Many of the entrepreneurs interviewed during fieldwork in the summer of 1996 expressed a strong interest in Western management. Two successful private business owners in Beijing were pursuing MBA degrees from the top programs in the country, while reading biographies of foreign entrepreneurs on the side. One computer scientist turned entrepreneur, subcontracting for Motorola in China, asked the interviewer to recommend some good books on corporate culture, since he was concerned about how to boost worker commitment and improve his company's image. Many of these entrepreneurs have relatives or former classmates who are now in business in the United States, Canada, Australia, or Hong Kong, so they can keep up with the latest trends there, even if at a distance.

THE ENVIRONMENT OF THE NEW ENTREPRENEUR

Private firms in China must exist in an environment where many resources are still controlled by the state. Yet especially at the local level in rural areas, this is a very different state; it is now almost desperate for resources. The county government's payroll in many places has more than doubled in the past decade (Blecher and Shue 1996),[1] and they are under continuous pressure to provide more jobs to the family members, relatives, or friends of those working in the government.[2]

The county government is also expected to improve the local infrastructure, education, and public health and safety, all of which require additional sources of revenue. At the lower level, township officials, although entitled to receiving salaries based on their rank, get more responsibilities from above without a corresponding increase in resource allocation. The village leaders are now responsible for their own payment and for their fellow villagers' cash income.

Fostering private enterprise can be one way out of this fiscal dilemma. One county official summarized three benefits of promoting private instead of public enterprises: "We put in no investment. We bear no risk. We collect taxes from them." Some localities make it easier to apply for a license to do business, often a complicated and time-consuming process, and allow the new firm to start business operations while applying for a license.

Capital, Land, Electricity, and Water

Once a business has started, it must navigate a series of other obstacles, most of which involve a knowledge of local power arrangements. Capital must be secured (usually from one's family or friends, or in rare cases, from a state bank), then land (or space), electricity, and water usually must be obtained. This can involve negotiations with local power holders (such as a village head), groups of villagers, or representatives of state bureaucracies.

In some cases, entrepreneurs have found it easier, cheaper, and less time-consuming to move their operations out of villages and into economic development zones in county towns. While they may have to pay a little more in wages and rent, they receive some guarantees about the availability of resources and do not have to keep renegotiating agreements or placating, often with cash, fresh groups of local citizens.

---

[1] One county official interviewed complained that the central government kept adding new responsibilities and functions to the local government without providing the necessary funding. In fact, many local staff members, including teachers, receive a portion or even all of their salaries from the revenues generated by the local government.

[2] The driver who took me to meet with entrepreneurs during my field trip said that he paid an "allocation fee" (*anpaifei*) of close to one-third of his annual income as a taxi driver to a county-owned factory in order to get a temporary job there; he later switched to the county government after a series of gift-giving.

Buying Raw Materials and Transportation

By 1994, prices for most consumer and producer products were no longer controlled by the government. The earlier two price tracks, market and administrative, had converged. For most private manufacturers, raw materials such as cotton, wood, bamboo, plastic, and steel now come directly from producers or markets at going rates. During the interviews, most entrepreneurs remarked that no special contacts were needed to purchase raw materials. In many cases, raw materials were from a spot (one-time sale) market. Entrepreneurs often preferred the spot market because it left them unconstrained by any obligation to buy from recurrent suppliers. Moreover, they were often able to demand a grace period for payments in what had become a buyers' market.

A similar trend also occurred in transportation. Since private transportation companies and individual truck drivers were allowed to compete with public transportation, there has been a rapid surge in private transportation services as a response to the shortage of supply and the low quality of services provided by public companies. Most business owners interviewed did not own a truck, or had sold their trucks, choosing instead to contract out their shipping tasks to private trucking companies since it was cheaper.

Reaching Customers and Markets

Depending on the level of market competition, entrepreneurs tended to adopt different strategies to reach customers. If the market competition was absent or limited, entrepreneurs did not have to worry about keeping up personal relationships with their customers. Five of the 32 entrepreneurs interviewed reported that they faced little market competition. Three of these were in high-technology development, and their products could not be easily copied.[3] The other two operated in markets that remained heavily regulated.

But in most cases, where production required few technological or capital inputs and market competition was intense, entrepreneurs had to maintain friendly relationships with buyers. Shared ascriptive ties such as kinship or common region and dialect, or relationships such as former schoolmates, comrades-in-arms, or work colleagues, often turned into trustworthy business relationships.

Entrepreneurs also sometimes discovered the "strength of weak ties" (Granovetter 1973), or the usefulness of keeping up social networks with people they hadn't seen for a long time. For example, some rural entrepreneurs maintained contact with the urban educated youth once sent down to their villages during the latter stages of the Cultural Revolution (1969–76). When these youth later returned to cities and occupied

---

[3] When asked whether he was planning to apply for a patent for his technological innovation, one entrepreneur said, "Definitely not. As soon as you put the process on paper, someone will get it and copy your invention."

key positions in large enterprises and government agencies, local entrepreneurs found them useful to gain access to subcontracting orders, needed capital, technology, information, and the urban market.

The Entrepreneurial Social Class

Contrary to what their distinctive lifestyle might suggest (see Chapter 8), private business owners in China do not identify themselves as a unique and independent social force. About 60 percent of the respondents in the entrepreneur sample reported that their closest relatives or friends were working in the state or urban collective sector, and 4 in 10 reported that their closest relative or friend was a government official. Many fewer reported having a closest relative or friend in the private sector. There was little evidence to suggest the emergence of a shared class identity. So even if in terms of income or consumption style there is a distinctive entrepreneurial class *in itself*, it is not yet a class *by itself*.

In addition, about 30 percent of the urban entrepreneurs' spouses were in the private sector, but 40 percent were still in the state or urban collective sector. For rural entrepreneurs, 36 percent of the spouses were in the private sector and 30 percent still in farming. Apparently not all entrepreneurs were determined to fully and continuously engage in the private sector. Rather, they tended to "leave one foot on another boat" by keeping their spouse or other family members in the more secure state sector or on the farm, thereby reducing entrepreneurial risk in a mixed economy. In a word, entrepreneurs in China were deeply embedded in their preexisting social relations and were far from being a full-fledged independent social force created by the market.

SUMMARY

Though there has been a phenomenal growth of a private sector economy in China since the beginning of economic reform, private businesses generally are still small and concentrated in the labor-intensive processing and service sectors. Yet unlike large state enterprises, which are still constrained by noneconomic factors such as the iron rice bowl, private firms are more autonomous and flexible and able to better respond to market forces.

There are three types of entrepreneurs: the rural *neng ren* (able person) were either farmers with special skills and nonfarm experiences or local officials with organizational skills and political connections to engage in vegetable or animal farming or orchard, transportation, or construction companies. The urban *dao ye* (master of profiteering) were those who, blocked from state sector jobs, took advantage of the high demand for certain consumer goods and services in cities by setting up restaurants, hair salons, and retail stores early in the reform era. The urban *xia hai* (go down to the sea of commerce) were later entrepreneurs with technical and managerial backgrounds who quit their state sector jobs and established private firms that utilized their specialties. Though entrepreneurs are far better off than the rest of the population in terms of economic status (income and lifestyle), they are still too unorganized and short-term oriented to be considered a unified class.

Evidence suggests that private business owners are gradually moving away from family management, which was often disruptive. However, it is naive to assume that private firms are able to eliminate all types of uncertainties and achieve high efficiency without minimum formal institutional guarantees and effective government actions to ensure a stable economic environment. Larger, capital-intensive, and high-technology firms and those facing greater market competition may soon exhaust their informal network resources and have to depend more on formal rules of business conduct. Therefore, as the private sector expands in China, more and more firms will reach the limit of these informal arrangements in providing certainty and trust; they will need an established and forcefully implemented universalistic code of conduct. China may even soon need the development of commercial law and, much to its chagrin, lawyers.

CHAPTER 11

Emerging Social Problems

China will face a variety of predictable and unpredictable problems over the next several decades. In this chapter, we will sketch out what we and a number of China experts see as key kinds of sociological problems. They have been divided into three major areas: problems related to the size and distribution of the population, problems related to the development of human resources, and tensions between state, local, and individual interests.

PROBLEMS OF THE SIZE, GROWTH, AND DISTRIBUTION OF THE POPULATION

As the world's largest nation (at least until India surpasses its population sometime in the early twenty-first century), China has unique problems. Its rapid economic development and the success of its population planning program over the last two decades have solved some of its more pressing problems. In some cases, these efforts have given China more breathing room in which to try to deal with its problems; in other cases, these apparent solutions have created new and serious problems themselves.

Will the State Be Able to Continue the Family Planning Program?

As was discussed in Chapter 6, the ability of the state to continue the One-Child Policy is of some concern. There are several interrelated questions here. Is the one-child policy absolutely necessary for continued economic growth or to put off ecological disaster? Is it possible that the Chinese birth rate would remain at much the same rate it is today with a different, and less oppressive, mix of inducements to keep births low? Finally, with the decline in the economic power of the state over households and individuals, will it be possible to maintain the one-child policy without moving to very coercive means of control (Skinner and Winkler 1969)?

We expect that in the prosperous rural areas of south and east China, the two-child policy (for that is what it really is) would probably continue even without government regulations. Changes in gender status, educational levels, and perceived opportunities for children's advancement all encourage families to have few children. We are less optimistic about poorer areas of rural China, especially in the north and west, where there are fewer opportunities for the betterment of children's social status and where educational levels of women may actually have declined over the past decade.

Who Will Take Care of the Elderly?

It may come as a surprise to realize that China is a rapidly aging nation. In 1995, only about 7 percent of the Chinese population was 65 years or older, and the ratio of elderly to those in the working ages (age 15–64) was about 6.5 elderly per 100 working-age people. The former measure shows the proportion of elderly in the total population; the latter shows the ratio of elderly to those upon whom they must be dependent, either directly or indirectly, for support. Banister (1992a) has projected the proportion of elderly and their ratio to the working-age population under two assumptions: (a) if China has an effective one-child policy from 1985 on, or (b) if Chinese couples give birth to an average of two children from 1985 on. If a one-child policy is effective, then by 2020, 15 percent of all Chinese will be elderly, and their ratio to the working-age population will be 19.2 elderly per 100 working-age people. By 2050, the elderly will be a whopping 41 percent of the population, and each 100 working-age people will be supporting 77 elderly. By way of contrast, the proportion of the elderly in the U.S. population was 12.8 percent in 1995 and is projected to rise to about 20.4 percent by 2050 (Anderton et al. 1997: 19).

If Chinese couples have two children rather than one, then Banister predicts that by 2020 12 percent of the population will be elderly, a proportion that will rise to 22 percent by 2050. Similarly, the ratio of elderly to working-age population will increase from 18 per 100 in 2020 to 36 per 100 in 2050. If China is successful in its one-child policy, it will have a huge group of elderly, most of whom are already born, who must be supported by a relatively small group of working-age adults. On the other hand, if a two-child policy prevails, the ratio of elderly to younger people will be lower, but of course the overall size of the population will be far larger (Zeng 1992).

These are the horns of the Chinese demographic dilemma. Is it better to have a smaller but extremely old population or a larger population with a more even distribution across ages? A very old population can put great demands on retirement and medical systems, as demographers who are projecting the impact of retirement of the baby boom generation in the United States (which will really start to hit about 2007) have discovered. On the other hand, China is a nation that is relatively poor in natural resources, including farmland. Would it be able to support the additional population that would be generated by a two-child rather than a one-child policy over the next several decades? The continuation of the one-child policy almost guarantees difficult social and government adaptations over the next several decades, but the two-child (or higher) policy could also prove disastrous from an economic and ecological point of view.

Even in urban areas, China is still a nation where the younger generation is expected, and compelled by law, to support their elders. Yet increasing life expectancy and the rise of the one-child family in cities means that the elderly, especially elderly women, now face a greater possibility of living out their declining years without either a spouse or a child to help them. Zeng Yi has projected 1986 birth, death, and marriage rates and estimated that in the future the "percentages of city women who are both childless and widowed are 4.9 percent and 11.0 percent at ages 75 and 85, respectively" (1991: 167). In a family-based society like China, these elderly family fragments may become a significant social problem.

Just as in the United States, the growing number of elderly in China will include many with health problems and disabilities. The shift in state responsibility for the provision of medical care to work units has led them to try to get consumers, often the elderly, to pay more of the cost. Paradoxically, because of the Medicare system, the United States is more socialist than China with regard to payment for medical care for the elderly. The elderly in China now have more fears and concerns about who will take care of them in their old age, especially if they have long and disabling diseases.

One result of this is a change in the nature of the intergenerational contract between older parents and their adult children (Ikels 1993: 307–33). Parents now recognize that since they may be more dependent on their children in old age, they should form a stronger bond of affection with them earlier on and not just rely on norms about filial piety to force children to obey them, even in adulthood. The current shift in resources away from the elderly and toward children may mean greater freedom for children in many areas, including choice of occupation and marriage partners.

There is also some indication that the burden of care for the elderly in Chinese cities is becoming more diffuse. Chinese elderly who lack a son report that they have just as much contact with and get just as much support from all their children as those who have a son (Bian et al. 1998). With more opportunities to change jobs and move to new areas, the expectation that older parents will live out their lives with one of their sons may have to change to a wider support network for the elderly.

Where Should New Urban Areas Be Located?

China's rapid industrial development over the past two decades has forced the government to decide where the infrastructure (roads, sewer lines, telephone systems, and so on) supporting this growth should be located. In many Third World nations, the infrastructure is often concentrated in a few large cities, and smaller towns and the countryside lag far behind.

China presents a different picture of infrastructure development. Before 1949, there was little development of infrastructure, and the new Communist state purposely tried to limit the growth of the largest cities. It tried to link population growth and economic development to the overall industrialization of the nation, often building up urban areas near sources of natural resources. During the 1960s, when the Chinese leadership was afraid of attack by both the United States and the Soviet Union, it attempted a "guerilla base" approach to urban infrastructure development, scattering cities and factories across China's vast hinterland to make it more difficult to cripple China by invasion of only a few key areas. By the late 1960s and early 1970s, decisions about industrial and infrastructure location were also influenced by political motives: The Gang of Four tried to place factory workers, who they thought were their most reliable supporters, near centers of political power by building factories outside Beijing and Shanghai.

China is now coming to grips with this economically illogical history of location of urban populations. Over the past two decades, a new factor has become important: China is now producing for the world market. Thus the development of new Chinese cities and towns is influenced by their communication with and proximity to the world market.

Early in the 1980s, China developed the new city of Shenzhen, just over the border from Hong Kong. It was to be an experimental city, designed to adapt Western technology to China but stripped of Western culture, which was often denounced as "spiritual pollution." To help redistribute industries linked to the world economy, China has begun to develop the infrastructure for two other huge projects. One is Pudong, a major, high-technology city on the outskirts of Shanghai. The other is the 'Round Bohai development zone, an attempt to link in the heavy industrial areas of the southern part of northeast China with Beijing, Tianjin, and rapidly developing urban areas of Shandong province. In addition, China is developing the world's largest hydroelectric project on the Chiang Jiang (Yangtze River) in western Sichuan province, the Three Gorges Project. These projects are attempts to avoid concentrating all of China's industries, especially its export and high-technology ones, in one part of the country.

As was mentioned in Chapter 9, China has also tried to develop towns and small cities in rural regions to reduce the pressure on major urban areas. These smaller cities and towns often have a better quality of life than big cities, and as they improve their infrastructure, they may become attractive to urbanites in the future.

What Will Happen to the Environment?

As was noted in Chapter 2, even as China has established one of the world's more successful, and draconian, family planning programs, its

While China is developing rapidly, it still depends heavily on animate energy sources and on coal for heating many city dwellings (see the black cylinders in the back of the pedicab).

population continues to grow. Many areas of China have suffered from overpopulation and environmental degradation for centuries. As a result of economic development, each person consumes many more resources than a few decades ago. While the growth of a consumer society in China will certainly make the average person's life more comfortable in the short run, it will have a major impact on the environment as well.

One major problem of rapidly industrializing Chinese cities, and of cities in many Third World nations, is that there is little zoning. Industrial sites emitting large amounts of pollution are often located next to residential areas. The huge death toll (in the hundreds of thousands) from the 1976 earthquake in the northern city of Tangshan was made much worse because coal mines that had been dug directly beneath the city collapsed.

Air pollution is rampant in most major Chinese cities and in many rural areas surrounding industrial sites as well. Lung cancer, due to air pollution and cigarette smoking, is common in every major industrial city. Water pollution is also widespread, both from untreated micro-organisms and from industrial and agricultural chemicals. In many areas of China, three sets of interests compete for water: industrial users, including chemical factories; urban consumers; and farmers. Virtually nowhere is tap water safe to drink. In recent years, the huge Huang He (Yellow River) has been drying up before it reaches the ocean; at times, armed guards have patrolled its banks for the last several hundred kilometers to prevent unsanctioned users, usually local farmers, from tapping its flow.

The history of environmental degradation during the twentieth century has shown that both capitalist and Communist regimes that place their highest priority on economic growth can do an equally appalling job at despoiling the natural world. Today in China there still is almost no legal protection for the environment or any means by which ordinary citizens can speak up. The huge Three Gorges Project, which will change the nature of several heavily populated provinces surrounding the upper Chang Jiang (the Yangtze River) forever, was undertaken with little or no concern for how it would affect the ecology of one of the world's great rivers.

HUMAN RESOURCE PROBLEMS

Despite a huge population, China will face significant problems in human resource development, not the least of which is that this area of study is almost unknown in China. The lack of attention to human resource development is of particular importance because it has the potential to exacerbate the widening gap between richer and poorer regions. It could also handicap China's future effort to move much of its workforce up from low-technology mass production to the more profitable medium- and high-technology sectors found in developed nations.

What Can Be Done to Improve the Educational System?

As was shown in Chapter 4, China faces very significant challenges in several areas of education. A large proportion of the population, especially women, in rural areas is illiterate or semiliterate. At present, this will have relatively little effect on production by unskilled workers, whether for the domestic or export market. Yet as labor becomes more scarce and the skills demanded increase, and as China tries to upgrade its technology, the low level of educational achievement of the population may begin to be important.

The college-educated population comprises less than one out of every hundred Chinese adults. So far, much of the growth of industry has been staffed by new college graduates or by shifting better-educated workers out of unproductive bureaucratic jobs. However, this latter source is not infinite; if China continues to grow at 8 to 10 percent per year, it may experience shortages of skilled and highly educated workers. China has shown reluctance to invest in the educational infrastructure, especially for higher education, that other nations have found necessary to compete in the high-technology world. So far, China has been able to avoid this kind of investment because it has such a large population; yet if it continues to grow at such a high rate, it may yet exhaust its resources of highly educated workers.

What about Massive Underemployment in Rural Areas?

The last several decades have shown that China, like many Third World nations, has a rural population that is far too large for the amount of available farmland (see the beginning of Chapter 9). When the household responsibility system brought back family farming to China after 1978, the nation saw remarkable increases in production. In some areas, farm families were able to produce twice as much as they had under communal farming methods. However, increases in productivity have slowed in the past decade. Increased production has begun to push down the prices for agricultural goods, making it less profitable for farmers to devote more hours of work to farm production.

A huge proportion of China's rural labor is redundant. Much labor is spent performing unnecessary tasks; in many cases, a job that one person could perform is divided among several just to keep everyone employed. Some agricultural economists in the early 1980s suggested that if as much as half of China's rural workforce vanished, the next year's crop would be about the same size as the last year's.

The surplus rural labor force also reduces pressures to make agriculture more technologically efficient, since mechanization can cause further loss of jobs. There is some evidence that rural industrial and agricultural development can actually lead to more out-migration, especially by farm laborers displaced by more efficient and less labor-intensive methods of farming (Zai and White 1997: 334–35). As in many Third World nations, farmers are reluctant to invest in agricultural machinery if they can get the job done just as cheaply by hiring someone, frequently a relative, from the locality. Thus the surplus labor force also hinders the emergence of a market for labor-saving agricultural machinery, most of which could be made in China.

This vast underemployed or semiemployed rural workforce is one of the major sources of workers for China's growing rural and urban factories, for its construction workforce, and for urban service industries (e.g., waiters to maids). This "reserve army of the underemployed" makes a huge potential workforce available to Chinese industry, virtually guaranteeing low labor costs for unskilled jobs and low prices for goods produced by unskilled labor.

Yet the surplus agricultural labor force is unevenly distributed across the nation. Jobs can often only be found through migration, which often causes social disruption and personal hardship in both the sending and receiving communities. These migrants, who often cannot become legal residents of the areas to which they have moved, must exist outside of the social safety net of the locality. This means little access to health and welfare services; in addition, that they want to escape police notice can make them easy prey for criminals, since crimes against them are much less likely to be reported.

TENSIONS BETWEEN THE STATE, LOCAL, AND INDIVIDUAL INTERESTS

How Will China Be Governed in the Future?

Some Chinese and Western intellectuals say that China will never de-velop into a Western-style democracy. These theorists point to China's long history of autocratic rule, to the fact that it is still an underdevel-oped nation, and to the vast and varied population that the government must control. Some of these theorists also maintain that Chinese child-rearing patterns, culture, and formal and informal social structures pro-vide little support for democratic principles. They say that many Chinese fear that freedom can easily degenerate into disorder and libertinism, and that Chinese feel more comfortable with a predictable, autocratic (or at least authoritarian) form of rule.

Some of these theorists are found among the current supporters of the governments of the People's Republic and Singapore; others simply see Chinese culture and social structure as poor soil in which the seeds of democratic institutions might grow. Leaving aside the obvious current political reasons why they would emphasize this point of view about Chinese, is there much evidence that democratic politics don't or can't work among Chinese?

Since the mid-1970s, both Taiwan and South Korea (a nation strongly influenced by Chinese cultural and political models for many centuries) have shown a rapid and pronounced turn toward democratic forms of government. Both have high levels of political participation, and both have recently shown that governments could even be turned out of office through democratic means. One problem of the cultural school of Chinese authoritarianism is that it fails to account for these developments. Yet Taiwan and Korea are far ahead of China in terms of levels of educa-tion and the proportion of the population that could be classified as mid-dle class; even the more enthusiatic supporters of democracy would admit that these two factors help to foster stable democratic institutions.

Since the student demonstrations in Tiananmen Square were put down in June 1989, it appears that the Communist Party is in firm control (Baum 1991). Yet there are a number of signs that what social scientists call a "civil society" may be emerging in China (Wakeman 1993). There is much less attempt by the government to control individual behavior in China today, and often those attempts are not all that effective. In many villages and towns, the local political authorities must respond to the will of the local people as much as to directives from above; and it has been es-timated that in perhaps half a million Chinese villages the village head is now elected. The emergence of a newly rich class provides a different mea-sure of social status besides political power. China today is a confusing place: "Puritans and philanderers now exist side by side; the point is that they are making their own decisions about private conduct, that there is such a thing as private conduct" (Kristof and WuDunn 1993: 299).

Can State Industries Be Made More Efficient?

Just as in rural communes and production brigades before 1978, there has been strong political pressure on Chinese state industries to generate employment for as many people as possible. This pressure was amplified by two other factors. Since China was virtually cut off from competition in most world markets for industrial goods for several decades before the early 1980s, there was little pressure on Chinese factories to keep up with advancing standards of technical complexity. Communist states never emphasized design or convenience in consumer goods, and such goods never had to meet the test of the market (whether anyone would buy them). As in other Communist states, a politically inspired shortage of consumer goods meant that there was a market for industrial goods, no matter how shoddy or nonfunctional.

This situation has changed dramatically: Now the pressure is on state industries to compete with private ones. One key question for China is whether these industries can be overhauled without massive layoffs and widespread bankruptcies. The workers in these industries are well organized and still have a significant amount of political power. They could disrupt the reform politics of the past few years if they were simply dumped out on the streets. Dealing with these state industries and their workers will be one of the Chinese leadership's greatest problems.

Will Regionalism Develop in China?

One of the most common observations about the process of economic development is that social and economic differentiation often becomes greatest in the early period of industrialization. Regions begin to specialize in one industry or another, often on the basis of what natural resource they have, and extremes of wealth and poverty are even greater during early industrialization (such as the robber baron era in the United States during the late nineteenth century) than they were before or after. This differentiation between regions, classes, and individuals can lead to conflict and political instability.

The post-1978 economic reforms have brought an uneven pattern of development to China. Foreign investment, a key engine of industrial development, has until recently been concentrated in the southern and eastern coastal provinces. Many of the northern and western provinces and autonomous regions, which are the primary source for natural resources such as coal or timber, still must provide these goods to the coastal provinces at prices set in the state five-year plans. Yet the citizens of these northern and western provinces must buy consumer goods at prevailing market prices, which are often far higher than before. As a result, the terms of trade between these two groups has changed, usually in favor of the coastal provinces and their entrepreneurs. The coal miner at a state-run mine in the western region of Ningxia is happy that there are now millionaires in Shanghai, but he is not pleased that his income has actually shrunk in terms of real purchasing power over the past decade (*The Wall Street Journal* June 1, 1998).

For a decade or two after the revolution of 1949, the Chinese people could be motivated to a remarkable amount of self-sacrifice toward the goal of economic development. There were two reasons for this. First, people were willing to sacrifice their own creature comforts (especially in terms of accepting substandard food, housing, and consumer goods) because the Communist Party promised that their sacrifice would mean that their children would have an easier life. Second, the Communist Party stressed that this sacrifice was shared. Since everyone was sacrificing to approximately the same degree, it was easier to live with privation.

Yet almost 50 years after 1949, the children of the revolution, who are now in their middle age, are much more cynical about the need for self-sacrifice and about the possible gains that will come from it. The mass media still emphasizes how workers and cadres should serve the people but now also touts entrepreneurs who have gotten rich. The Chinese population, young people in particular, now get a very mixed message about the fundamental values of their society.

One might argue that this conflict exists in many societies, including our own. Is it better to be an ill-paid minister or social worker or a rich stockbroker? Who contributes more to society? In American society, the rich at least partially justify their role by making charitable donations and serving in various volunteer capacities. One key question in China in the future will be what groups are perceived as having the greatest or most legitimate claim to leadership and power, and how will they use it.

Webliography

Internet resources on China are expanding rapidly, both in Chinese and in other languages. The sites listed below give an introduction to some of the resources available on the World Wide Web. Many Chinese universities, cities, and provinces now have their own Web sites and can be found using Internet search engines.

Internet Guides on China

Australian National University: Library Sites on China
http://online.anu.edu.su/Asia/Chi/ChiLib.html

Heidelberg University (Germany) Internet Guide for Chinese Studies
http://www.cnd.org/mirror/netguide/ngmain.htm

University of Vienna (Austria) China Virtual Library
http://www.univie.ac.at/Sinologie/netguide.htm

General Directory on China

http://www.nihao.com

Information on Scholarly Publications and Conferences on China

Australian National University Chinese Studies Bulletin
http://online.anu.edu.au/Asia/Chi/ChiBull.html

Chinese Government Sources

"China ABC" from Embassy of the People's Republic of China in Washington, DC
http://www.china-embassy.org/China/China.htm

U.S. Government Sources

U.S. Army Area Handbook on China
http://www-chaos.umd.edu/history/handbook.html

Geographic, Social, and Economic Data on China

China in Space and Time (CITAS) Project, University of Washington
http://citas.csde.washington.edu

Chinese Culture and Art

China the Beautiful Web site
http:/www.chinapage.com/china.html

Women in China

Materials on China from the United Nations' Fourth World
Conference on Women, 1996
http:/ss5ihep.ac.cn/women/cwomen.html

Hong Kong

Hong Kong Government Web site
http:/www.geocities.com.Tokyo/Towers/2464/government.htm

Tibet (Xizang Autonomous Region)

University of Vienna (Austria), Tibet WWW Virtual Library
http:/ciolek.com/WWWVL-TibetanStudies.html

GLOSSARY

activists   People who took an enthusiastic part in campaigns led by the Communist Party and who might be groomed for eventual membership in the party.

ancestor worship   Chinese religious rituals whereby the ancestors would be honored by different kinds of offerings at various times of the year. These rites also stressed the importance of having at least one surviving male in the younger generation to carry on the family name.

Bamboo Wall   The prohibition of rural-to-urban migration through the use of the household registration system (the *hu kou*).

bourgeoisie   Those with capital, that is those with ownership of the means of production.

bureaucracy   A form of organization based on rules, written directions, hierarchy, merit-based promotion, and specialization of functions.

cadre   A leader, usually a Communist Party member, who helps to accomplish party objectives.

campaigns   Periodic political movements in China designed to prevent the population from slipping into a bureaucratic routine. They were also a way to encourage concrete demonstrations of ideological commitment through working extra hours, taking on undesirable tasks, exposing hidden enemies, and so on.

class label   Until the late 1970s, each citizen of China was put in a category based on his or her pre-1949 family background: landlord, poor peasant, worker, and so on. Until the late 1970s, one's life chances were heavily determined by one's class background.

cohort   A group of people who share a demographic characteristic, such as all those born in 1948 or all women married in 1991.

Confucianism   A system of thought following the precepts of philosopher Kong Zi (551–479 BC) that emphasized the importance of stability and hierarchy in social relations.

contract responsibility system   A component of urban economic reform of the late 1970s in which decision making was delegated to factory managers.

Cultural Revolution   The campaign started by Mao Zedong in 1966 to level Chinese society and make every institution into an instrument of revolutionary ideology; ended with Mao's death in 1976.

dakuan   The new, rich entrepreneurs (post-1979).

danwei   The work unit; a generic term for government agencies, state enterprises, and other organizations that provide a wide variety of services for their employees.

Daoism   An ancient Chinese philosophy that emphasizes adapting to the changes inherent in nature.

developed nations   Nations that make extensive use of inanimate sources of power and have a highly specialized division of labor; their citizens are in frequent contact with distant places.

division of labor   The process by which societies divide work into specialized tasks—the butcher, the baker, the candlestick maker.

entrepreneurs   Those who discover new ways of combining labor, resources, and technology and often become rich by doing so.

female infanticide   The murder of female infants, practiced throughout Chinese history to some degree. After the advent of the one-child policy in 1979, families had an even greater reason to do away with a girl if it would prevent them from giving birth to a male infant.

feudalism   The social system of rural hierarchies (kings, knights, serfs, and so on) that preceded the rise of capitalism in the West. In China, the term is used in a less precise way to describe pre-1949 social relations.

Four Modernizations   Deng Xiaoping's 1978 policy to modernize China in agriculture, industry, national defense, and science and technology. This policy led to much more contact with the outside world.

Gang of Four   A clique of four leaders (including Mao's wife, Jiang Qing) who launched campaigns against Deng Xiaoping and other rightists in the latter stages of the Cultural Revolution. They fell from power one month after Mao's death in 1976.

getihu   Post-1979 self-employed households; many later grew into privately owned businesses.

grand or extended family   A coresident family composed of grandparents, two or more brothers, and the brothers' wives and children.

Great Leap Forward   Attempt by Mao Zedong in 1958 to greatly increase industrial and agricultural production through use of huge work units (people's communes) and ideological fervor; ended with mass starvation (1959–61) in many regions.

guanxi   Social connections or networks that are extensively used to facilitate all types of social activities.

Han   The majority nationality in China, constituting about 93 percent of the population.

household responsibility system   The rural de-collectivization of the late 1970s that restored households as the key unit of production and consumption.

hu kou: The household registration system used for social control in China.

ideal type   Sociological concepts that have identifiable characteristics and are applicable to a number of cases. For example, the People's Liberation Army and the Illinois Department of Motor Vehicles are both bureaucracies because they have written rules, hierarchical organization, and so on.

iron rice bowl (*tie fan wan*) The permanent employment system at state enterprises and government agencies that prevents employees from being fired.

labor market In market-based economies, the process by which employers and potential employees decide on hiring arrangements.

land reform campaign The 1950–53 overthrow of traditional Chinese landlord-tenant relations by a system whereby landlords were declared class enemies (and frequently executed) and the state controlled all farmland.

latent function A social arrangement that has a hidden, and sometimes unintended or unrecognized effect.

less-developed nations Countries that still make considerable use of animate sources of energy, have a large proportion of their populations in agriculture, and whose citizens have few contacts beyond their family and town or village.

life expectancy at birth The mean number of years that a member of a population is expected to live given a specified set of age-specific mortality rates.

Maoism The particular version of Marxism developed by Mao Zedong, influenced by the thought of Lenin, Stalin, and his own revolutionary experiences in rural China.

marriage market The process by which families, or individuals, choose marriage partners.

models Individuals or work units that become symbolic of certain virtues; often highly publicized during campaigns.

modernization The process by which the social, economic, and political institutions needed to sustain and promote advanced industrial activities are developed.

national minorities Minority groups (55) with distinctive languages and customs, comprising about 7 percent of China's population; more heavily concentrated in the west and south.

Nationalist Party (*Kuomintang*) The political party that ruled China from the 1920s until 1949. It ruled only Taiwan after that date, first as a dictatorship, more recently as one of several competing parties in one of Asia's most democratic legislatures.

nuclear family A coresident family composed of husband, wife, and their minor children.

One-Child Policy The 1979 policy that restricted Chinese urban couples to only one child and Chinese rural couples to only one son.

Overseas Chinese Communities of Chinese, and their descendants, who live outside of China; they are most numerous in Southeast Asia, the United States, Australia, and Canada.

planned economy An economic system based on state ownership of productive resources and bureaucratic coordination of production and consumption processes.

production brigade   From the mid-1950s to 1978, a key unit of agricultural administration, usually equivalent to the size of the old natural village, usually about 250–1,500 people.

production team   From the mid-1950s to 1978, the basic unit (usually of 10–30 households) of Chinese rural life with control over decisions about production and consumption.

professions   Occupational groups that have a monopoly on the ways in which their work is conducted and over the training and certification of new members.

putonghua   Sometimes called Mandarin, this northern dialect of Chinese is the official spoken language of China.

responsibility system   *See household responsibility system.*

sex ratio   The number of males divided by the number of females in a group; such as the sex ratio at birth or at age 65 and above.

social equality   The degree to which members of a society have similar access to resources and to opportunities for social mobility.

social mobility   Change of position in the system of social stratification, either within a single generation or between generations.

Special Economic Zones   Several cities along China's southeast coast that have tax incentives to encourage foreign investment and technological improvement.

stem family   A coresident family composed of one set of grandparents, one of their children and his or her spouse, and the grandchildren.

thought reform   A technique used by the Chinese Communists to try to convert nonbelievers or deviant thinkers to Maoist orthodoxy; often involved criticism and self-criticism and the use of violence or deprivation against recalcitrant individuals.

Three Bitter Years   Period (1959–61) of starvation in rural China following the failure of the Great Leap Forward; 30–35 million extra Chinese may have died in this era.

Tiananmen Square   A very large paved area in central Beijing bordering many major buildings and monuments; site of the June 3–4, 1989, massacre of students and workers by the Twenty-seventh Army and other units of the People's Liberation Army.

total institutions   Institutions in which almost all activities of the inmates can be controlled, such as prison or military boot camps. Often total institutions are directed at the attitude change of those within them.

work unit   See *danwei.*

REFERENCES

Ambrose, Stephen E. *Undaunted Courage: Meriwether Lewis, Thomas Jefferson and the Opening of the American West.* New York: Simon and Schuster, 1997.

Anderton, Douglas L., and Richard E. Barrett. "Demographic Seasonality and Development: The Effects of Agricultural Colonialism in Taiwan, 1906–42." *Demography* 27(1990), pp. 387–411.

Anderton, Douglas L., Richard E. Barrett, and Donald J. Bogue. *The Population of the United States.* New York: Free Press, 1997.

Andors, Phyllis. *The Unfinished Liberation of Chinese Women, 1949–1980.* Bloomington, IN: Indiana University Press, 1983.

Ashton, Basil, Kenneth Hill, Alan Piazza, and Robin Zeitz. "Famine in China, 1958–61." *Population and Development Review* 19 (1984) pp. 613–45.

Aziz, Sartaj. *Rural Development: Learning from China.* New York: Holms and Meier, 1978.

Banister, Judith. *China's Changing Population.* Palo Alto, CA: Stanford University Press, 1987.

Banister, Judith. "Implications of the Aging of China's Population." In *The Population of Modern China,* eds. Dudley L. Poston, Jr., and David Yaukey, pp. 463–90. New York: Plenum, 1992a.

Banister, Judith. "China's Changing Mortality." In *The Population of Modern China,* eds., Dudley L. Poston, Jr., and David Yaukey, pp. 163–224. New York: Plenum, 1992b.

Banister, Judith. "Ethnic Diversity and Distribution." In *The Population of Modern China,* eds., Dudley L. Poston, Jr., and David Yaukey, pp. 553–72. New York: Plenum, 1992c.

Barclay, George W. *Colonial Development and Population in Taiwan.* Princeton, NJ: Princeton University Press, 1954.

Barclay, G.W., A.J. Coale, M.A Stoto, and T.J. Trussell. " A Reassessment of the Demography of Traditional China." *Population Index* 42(1976), pp. 606–35.

Barrett, Richard E. "Short-Term Trends in Bastardy in Taiwan." *Journal of Family History* 5(1980), pp. 293– 312.

———. "Share Tenancy and Fixed Rent in Taiwan." *Economic Development and Cultural Change* 32(1984), pp. 413–22.

Barrett, Richard E., and Martin K. Whyte. "Dependency Theory and Taiwan: Analysis of a Deviant Case." *American Journal of Sociology* 87(1982), pp. 1064–89.

Barrett, Richard E., William P. Bridges, Moshe Semyonov, and Xiaoyuan Gao. "Female Labor Force Participation in China: An Ecological Analysis of Data from the 1982 Census of Population." *Rural Sociology* 56 (1991), pp. 1–21.

Barrett, Richard E., Yanchun Xu, and Barbara Zusman. "Trends in Arranged Marriage in China." Pp. 99–132 in George T. Yu, ed. *China in Transition.* Lanham, MD: University Press of America, 1993.

Baum, Richard, ed. *Reform and Reaction in Post-Mao China: The Road to Tiananmen Square.* New York: Routledge, 1991.

Benenson, Abram S., ed. *Control of Communicable Diseases Manual.* Washington, DC: American Public Health Association, 1995.

Bian, Fuqin, John R. Logan, and Yanjie Bian. "Intergenerational Relations in Urban China: Proximity, Contact, and Help to Parents." *Demography* 35(1998), pp. 115–24.

Bian, Yanjie. *Work and Inequality in Urban China.* Albany, NY: State University of New York Press, 1994.

Bian, Yanjie, and Soon Ang. "Guanxi Networks and Job Mobility in China and Singapore." Paper presented at the East Asia Workshop, the University of Chicago, 1996.

Bletcher, Marc, and Vivienne Shue. *Tethered Deer: Government and Economy in a Chinese Village.* Stanford, CA: Stanford University Press, 1996.

Buck, John Lossing. *The Chinese Farm Economy.* Chicago: University of Chicago Press, 1937.

Burgess, John. *The Guilds of Peking.* New York: Columbia University Press, 1928.

Buroway, Michael, and Peter Krotov. "The Soviet Transition from Socialism to Capitalism: Worker Control and Economic Bargaining in the Wood Industry." *American Sociological* Review 57(1992), pp.16–38.

Byrd, William A., and Lin Qingsong. *China's Rural Industry: Structure, Development and Reform.* Washington, DC: The World Bank, 1990.

Calhoun, Craig. *Neither Gods nor Emperors: Students and the Struggle for Democracy in China.* Berkeley: University of California Press, 1995.

Cheng, Nien. *Life and Death in Shanghai.* New York: Grove Press, 1986.

Chicago Tribune. "China May End Bureaucratic Paradise." March 6, 1998, pp. A-1, 24.

———. "China's Voluntary One-Child Policy Birthing New Revolution." May 24, 1998, pp. A-1, 14.

———. "Women's Rights Advocates Describe Plight, Successes."June 28, 1998, pp. A-12.

Cho, Lee-Jay. "Population Dynamics and Policy in China." In *The Population of Modern China,* eds. Dudley L. Poston, Jr., and David Yaukey, pp. 59–82. New York: Plenum, 1992.

Clough, Ralph. *Island China.* Cambridge, MA: Harvard University Press, 1982.

Coale, Ansley J. *Rapid Population Growth in China, 1952–1982.* Committee on Population and Demography, National Research Council, Report No. 27. Washington, DC: National Academy Press, 1984.

Connor, Walter D. "The Rocky Road: Entrepreneurship in the Soviet Economy, 1986–1989." In *The Culture of Entrepreneurship,* ed. Brigitte Berger, pp. 189–209. San Francisco, CA: ICS Press, 1991.

Croll, Elisabeth. *The Politics of Marriage in Contemporary China.* Cambridge: Cambridge University Press, 1981.

Davis, Deborah, and Stevan Harrell, eds. *Chinese Families in the Post-Mao Era.* Berkeley, CA: University of California Press, 1993.

Davis-Friedman, Deborah. *Long Lives: Chinese Elderly and the Communist Revolution.* Cambridge: Harvard University Press, 1983.

DeGlopper, Donald R. "The Social System." Pp. 97-150 in Federal Research Division (Library of Congress), *China: A Country Study.* Washington, DC: U.S. Government Printing Office, 1988.

Editorial Committee for the Atlas of Cancer Mortality. *Atlas of Cancer Mortality in the People's Republic of China.* Beijing: China Map Press, 1979.

Ellman, Michael. *Socialist Planning.* New York: Cambridge University Press, 1989.

Far Eastern Economic Review. "The Price of Progress." April 10, 1997, pp. 42–44.

———. "New Chinese Man." April 17, 1997, pp. 30–31.

————. "Workers' Offensive." May 29, 1997, pp. 50–52.

————. "The Burden of Age." October 23, 1997, pp. 82–84.

————. "Cracks in the Ceiling." October 23, 1997, pp. 85–86.

————. "The Red Bourgeoisie." November 27, 1997, p. 7.

Federal Research Division (Library of Congress). *China: A Country Study.* Washington, DC: U.S. Government Printing Office, 1988.

Fei, Hsiao-tung and Chih-I Chang. *Earthbound China.* London: Routledge and Kegan Paul Ltd. 1948.

Fei, John C., Gustav Ranis, and Shirley W.Y. Kuo. *Growth with Equity: The Taiwan Case.* New York: Oxford University Press, 1979.

Flinn, Michael W. 1981. *The European Demographic System.* Baltimore, MD: Johns Hopkins University Press, 1981.

Gates, Hill. "Cultural Support for Birth Limitation among Urban Capital-Owning Women." In *Chinese Women in the Post-Mao Era,* eds., Deborah Davis and Stevan Harrell, pp. 251–76. Berkeley: University of California Press, 1993.

Granovetter, Mark S. "The Strength of Weak Ties." *American Journal of Sociology* 78 (1973), pp. 1360–80.

Heng, Liang, and Judith Shapiro. *Son of the Revolution.* New York: Knopf, 1983.

Henriot, Christian. "'La Fermeture': The Abolition of Prostitution in Shanghai, 1949–58." *China Quarterly* 142 (1995), pp. 467–88.

Ho, Ping-ti. *The Population of China.* Chicago: University of Chicago Press, 1959.

Horowitz, Irving Louis. *C. Wright Mills: An American Utopian.* New York: Free Press, 1983.

Hsieh, Winston. "Migrant Peasant Workers in China: The PRC's Rural Crisis in an Historical Perspective." In *China in Transition,* ed., George T. Yu, pp. 89–98. Lanham, MD: University Press of America, 1993.

Ikels, Charlotte. "Settling Accounts: The Intergenerational Contract in an Age of Reform." In *Chinese Families in the Post-Mao Era,* eds., Deborah Davis and Stevan Harrell, pp. 307–333. Berkeley: University of California Press, 1993.

Jiang, Liu, Lu Xueyi, and Dan Tianlun, eds. *China in 1994–1995: Analysis and Forecast of Social Situation.* Beijing: China Social Science Press, 1995.

Johnson, Kay Ann. *Women, the Family and Peasant Revolution in China.* Chicago: University of Chicago Press, 1983.

Kaple, Deborah A. *Dream of a Red Factory: The Legacy of High Stalinism in China.* New York: Oxford University Press, 1994.

Kornai, Janos. *Socialist System: The Political Economy of Communism.* Princeton, NJ: Princeton University Press, 1992.

Kristof, Nicholas D., and Sheryl WuDunn. *China Wakes: The Struggle for the Soul of a Rising Power.* New York: Vintage, 1994.

LaCroix, Sumner, and Michael Plummer. *Emerging Patterns of East Asian Investment in China.* From Korea, Taiwan and Hong Kong. Armonk, NY; M.E. Sharpe, 1995.

Laumann, Edward O., John H. Gagnon, Robert T. Michaels, and Stuart Michaels. The *Social Organization of Sexuality: Sexual Practices in the United States.* Chicago: University of Chicago Press, 1994.

Li, Fang. "The Social Origins of Entrepreneurship: The Rise of Private Firms in China." Ph.D. thesis, Sociology Department, University of Chicago, 1997.

Li, Muzhen. "Distribution of Chinese Population." In *The Population of Modern China,* eds., Dudley L. Poston, Jr., and David Yaukey, pp. 83–112. New York: Plenum, 1992.

Lieberthal, Kenneth. "The Great Leap Forward and the Split in the Yan'an Leadership, 1958–65." In *The Politics of China*, 2nd ed, ed., Roderick MacFarquhar, pp. 87–147. Cambridge, England: Cambridge University Press, 1997.

Lifton, Robert J. *Thought Reform and the Psychology of Totalism.* New York: W.W. Norton, 1969.

Lin, Nan, and Yanjie Bian. "Getting Ahead in Urban China." *American Journal of Sociology* 97 (1991), pp. 657-88.

Lindblom, Charles E. *Politics and Markets.* New York: Basic Books, 1977.

Lipset, Seymour Martin. *American Exceptionalism: A Double-Edged Sword.* New York: W.W. Norton, 1996.

Liu, Dalin. *Zhongguo dangdai xing wenhua* (Sexual Behavior in Modern China: A Report of a Nationwide Sex Civilization Survey of 20,000 Subjects in China). Shanghai: Sanlian Shudian, 1992.

———. *Zhongguo gudai xing wenhua* (The Sex Culture of Ancient China). Yingchuan, Ningxia: Ningxia People's Press, 1993.

Liu, Gordon, Xingshu Liu, and Qingyue Meng. "Privatization of the Medical Market in Socialist China: A Historical Approach." *Health Policy* 27 (1994), pp. 157–74.

Lu, Xueyi. *Dangdai zhongguo nongcun yu dangdai zhongguo nongmin* (Rural Society and Peasants in Modern-Day China). Beijing: Zhishi Chubanshe, 1991.

Milor, Vedat, ed. *Changing Political Economies: Privatization in Post-Communist and Reforming Communist States.* Boulder and London: Lynne Rienner Publishers, 1994.

Naughton, Barry. "Implications of the State Monopoly over Industry and Its Relaxation." *Modern China* 18 (1992), pp. 14–41.

———. *Growing out of the Plan: Chinese Economic Reform, 1978–1993.* New York: Cambridge University Press, 1995.

Oi, Jean C. "Fiscal Reform and the Economic Foundation of Local Corporatism in China." *World Politics* 45 (1992), pp. 99–126.

Palmer, Michael. "The Re-emergence of Family Law in Post-Mao China: Marriage, Divorce and Reproduction." *China Quarterly* 141 (1995), pp. 110–34.

Pan, Suimin. *Zhongguo xing xianzhuang* (Sexuality in Contemporary China). Beijing: Guangming Daily Publishing House, 1995.

Parish, William L., "Introduction." In *Chinese Rural Development: The Great Transformation*, ed. William L. Parish, pp. 1–26. Armonk, NY: M.E Sharpe, 1985.

Parish, William L., and Martin King Whyte. *Village and Family in Contemporary China.* Chicago: University of Chicago Press, 1978.

Parish, William L., Xiaoye Zhe, and Fang Li. "Nonfarm Work and Marketization of the Chinese Countryside." *China Quarterly* 143 (1995) pp. 697–730.

People's Daily. "China among Top Ten in the World in Some Major Socioeconomic Indicators." March 3, 1998, p.1.

People's Daily, Overseas Edition. December 3, 1994, p.1.

Perkins, Dwight. "Reforming China's Economic System." *Journal of Economic Literature* 26 (1988), pp. 601–45.

Population Census Office. *Tabulation on the 1990 Population Census of the People's Republic of China, Volume 1.* Beijing: China Statistical Publishing House, 1993a.

———. *Tabulation on the 1990 Population Census of the People's Republic of China, Volume 2.* Beijing: China Statistical Publishing House, 1993b.

Poston, Dudley L., Jr. "Epilogue: China in 1990." In *The Population of Modern China*, eds., Dudley L. Poston, Jr., and David Yaukey, pp. 699–718. New York: Plenum, 1992.

Poston, Dudley L., Jr., and Shu Jing. "The Demographic and Socioeconomic Composition of China's Ethnic Minorities." *Population and Development Review* 13(1987), pp. 703–22.

Poston, Dudley L., Jr., and Mei-yu Yu. "The Distribution of the Overseas Chinese." In *The Population of Modern China*, eds. Dudley L. Poston, Jr. and David Yaukey, pp. 117–48. New York: Plenum, 1992.

Rabushka, Alvin. *The New China: Comparative Economic Development in Mainland China, Taiwan, and Hong Kong.* Boulder, CO: Westview, 1987.

Ragin, Charles, and David Zaret. 1983. "Theory and Method in Comparative Strategies." *Social Forces.* 61:731–754.

Richmond, Caroline. "China Is Now Moving Towards the Western Way of Death." *Canadian Medical Association Journal* 145 (1991), pp. 707–8.

Robinson, J.C. "Of Women and Washing Machines: Employment, Housework and Reproduction of Motherhood in Socialist China." *China Quarterly* 101 (1985), pp. 32-57.

Savada, Andrea M., and Ronald E. Dolan. "Education and Culture." In *China: A Country Study.* Federal Research Division (Library of Congress). Pp. 151–204. Washington, DC: U.S. Government Printing Office. 1988.

Schurmann, Franz H. *Ideology and Organization in Communist China.* Berkeley: University of California Press, 1968.

Shan, Guangnai. *Zhongguo changji–guochu he xianzai* (Prostitution in China–Past and Present). Beijing: Law Publishing House, 1995.

Shinn, Rinn-Sup, and Robert L. Worden. "Historical Setting." In *China: A Country Study.* Federal Research Division (Library of Congress). Pp. 1–58. Washington, DC: U.S. Government Printing Office, 1988.

Skinner, G. William. "Marketing and Social Structure in Rural China," Parts I–III. *Journal of Asian Studies* 1 (1964), pp. 3–43, 2 (1964), pp.195–228, 3 (1965), pp. 363–99.

Skinner, G. William, and Edwin A. Winkler. "Compliance Cycles in Rural China: A Cyclical Theory." In *A Sociological Reader on Complex Organizations*, 2nd ed, ed., Amitai Etzioni, pp. 410–38. New York: Holt, Rinehart and Winston, 1969.

Smelser, Neil J.. *Comparative Methods in the Social Sciences.* Englewood Cliffs, N.J.: Prentice-Hall, 1976.

Spence, Jonathan D. *The Search for Modern China.* New York: W.W. Norton, 1990.

Stacey, Judith. *Patriarchy and Socialist Revolution in China.* Berkeley: University of California Press, 1983.

State Statistical Bureau. *China Statistical Yearbook, 1992.* Beijing: China Statistical Publishing House, 1992.

———. *China Statistical Yearbook, 1995.* Beijing: China Statistical Publishing House, 1995a.

———. *Urban Statistical Yearbook of China.* Beijing: China Statistical Publishing House, 1995b.

Szelényi, Iván. *Urban Inequalities under State Socialism.* New York: Oxford University Press, 1983.

———."Eastern Europe in an Epoch of Transition: Toward a Socialist Mixed Economy?" In *Remaking the Economic Institutions of Socialism: China and Eastern Europe*, eds., Victor Nee and David Stark, pp. 209–32. Stanford, CA: Stanford University Press, 1989.

Tawney, R.H. *Land and Labor in China.* London: George Allen and Unwin, 1932, [reprinted by M.E. Sharpe, Inc., 1966].

Teiwes, Frederick C. "The Establishment and Consolidation of the New Regime, 1949–57." In *The Politics of China*, 2nd ed, ed., Roderick MacFarquhar, pp. 5–86. Cambridge, England: Cambridge University Press, 1997.

Thornton, Arland, and Hui-sheng Lin. *Social Change and the Family in Taiwan*. Chicago: University of Chicago Press, 1994.

U.S. Bureau of the Census. *Statistical Abstract of the United States*. Washington, DC: U.S. Government Printing Office, 1996.

Vogel, Ezra F. *One Step Ahead: Guangdong under Reform*. Cambridge, MA: Harvard University Press, 1989.

Wakeman, Jr., Frederic. "The Civil Society and Public Sphere Debate." *Modern China* 19(1993): pp.108–38.

Walder, Andrew G. *Communist Neotraditionalism: Work and Authority in Chinese Industry*. Berkeley: University of California Press, 1986.

———. "Property Rights and Stratification in Socialist Redistributive Economies." *American Sociological Review* 57, (1992), pp. 524–39.

———. "Local Governments as Industrial Firms: An Organizational Analysis of China's Transitional Economy." *American Journal of Sociology* 101(1995), pp. 263-301.

Wall Street Journal. "Beijing to Encourage Home Ownership." A-13.

———. "In China's Hinterlands, Rising Unemployment Spurs Stock Offerings." June 1, 1998. pp. A-1, 8.

Watson, Rubie, and Patricia Ebrey, eds. *Marriage and Inequality in Chinese Society*. Berkeley: University of California Press, 1990.

Welsh, Frank. *A Borrowed Place: The History of Hong Kong*. New York: Kodansha, 1996.

Whyte, Martin K. *Small Groups and Political Rituals in China*. Berkeley: University of California Press, 1972.

———. "Bureaucracy and Modernization in China: The Maoist Critique." *American Sociological Review* 38(1973), pp. 149–63.

———. "Changes in Mate Choice in Chengdu." In *Chinese Society on the Eve of Tiananmen: The Impact of Reform*, eds., Deborah Davis and Ezra F. Vogel, pp. 181–214. Cambridge: Harvard University Press, 1990.

Whyte, Martin K., and William L. Parish. *Urban Life in Contemporary China*. Chicago: University of Chicago Press, 1984.

Wittfogel, Karl. *Oriental Despotism*. New Haven, CT: Yale University Press, 1957.

Wittwer, Sylvan. *Feeding a Billion: Frontiers of Chinese Agriculture*. East Lansing, MI: Michigan State University Press, 1987.

Wolf, Margery. *Women and the Family in Rural Taiwan*. Stanford, CA: Stanford University Press, 1972.

———. *Revolution Postponed: Women in Contemporary China*. Stanford, CA: Stanford University Press, 1985.

Wolf, Margery, and Roxane Witke, eds. 1975. *Women in Chinese Society*. Stanford: Stanford, University Press, 1975.

Wong, Sui-Lun. *Emigrant Entrepreneurs: Shanghai Industrialists in Hong Kong*. Hong Kong: Oxford University Press, 1988.

Yang, C.K. *Chinese Communist Society: The Family and the Village*. Cambridge, MA: MIT Press, 1965.

Yang, Dali L. *Calamity and Reform in China*. Stanford, CA: Stanford University Press, 1996.

Yue, C.S. "The Role of Foreign Trade and Investment in the Development of Singapore" In *Foreign Trade and Investment: Economic Development in the Newly Industrializing Asian Countries,* ed. Walter Galenson, pp. 178–230. Madison, WI: University of Wisconsin Press, 1985.

Zai, Liang, and Michael J. White. "Market Transition, Government Policies, and Interprovincial Migration in China: 1983–1988." *Economic Development and Cultural Change* 45 (1997), pp. 321-39.

Zeng Yi. *Family Dynamics in China: A Life Table Analysis.* Madison, WI: University of Wisconsin Press, 1991.

———. "Changes in Family Structure in China" In *The Population of Modern China,* eds., Dudley L. Poston, Jr., and David Yaukey, pp. 535-47. New York: Plenum, 1992.

Zweig, David. *Agrarian Radicalism in China, 1968-1981.* Cambridge, MA: Harvard University Press, 1989.

NAME INDEX

SUBJECT INDEX

A

abortion, 26–27, 65
activists, 33, 35, 119
administrative areas, 8–10
Afghanistan, 6
Africa, 5
aging of the population, 26, 136–137
agricultural labor supply, 115
Agricultural Producers' Cooperatives, 30
agricultural production, 113–114
agriculture, 30, 141
American children, 43
American west, 5
ancestor worship, 10–11, 56
Anhui Village, 102
Anti-Rightist Campaign, 30, 37–38
apartments, 105–106
ascriptive label, 40
Australia, 5
authoritarian state, 4
automobiles, 106

B

baby boom, 112, 108
bad class background, 119
Bamboo Wall, 95, 111
bao-jia system, 60
behavior, 46
Beijing, 108
Beijing Jeep, 106
Bhutan, 6
birth planning, 2, 26, 135, 138
Bohai Gulf, 6
Bohai, 'Round, 138
bourgeoisie, 34
Brazil, 1
British empire, 4
bureaucratic control, 113
Burma, 6

C

cadres, 33–34
campaigns, 22, 30–32, 37–38, 47, 93
Canada, 5

cancer, 23–24, 84, 139
censuses, 20, 50
characters, Chinese, 13, 42, 46, 50
Chiang Jiang (Yangtze river), 6, 138, 140
Chicago, 5, 102
child care, 44, 89
child socialization, 37, 43–46
Chinese New Year, 45, 66
chronic diseases, 22
Chrysler Cherokee, 106
cities, 96–109
city dwellers, 103–104
city subdivisions, 98
Civil War (1946–49), 97
clans, 59, 69
class, 35–36, 107
class background, 40
class enemies, 33, 35
class label, 40
climate, 6
coercion, 65
cohorts, 52
Cold War, 87
collective farming, 113
collective sector, 90
collectivization, agricultural, 112–113
college graduates, 51–52
communes, 7, 30, 113
Communist asceticism, 78–79
Communist Party, 15, 31–34, 78, 84, 87–88, 93, 119, 142, 144
comrade, 41–42
concubines, 77
Confucian thought, 71–72, 76–77, 84, 124
Confucianism, 11, 55–57
Connecticut, 3
consumer goods, 100–101, 143, 144
consumption, 61
contract responsibility system, 116
contract workers, 102
control, 35, 79
corruption, 108, 117
cosmopolitanism, 107